EDITH WHARTON

EDITH WHARTON

A House Full of Rooms: Architecture, Interiors, and Gardens

THERESA CRAIG
Special Photography by John Bessler

THE MONACELLI PRESS

First published in the United States of America in 1996 by
The Monacelli Press, Inc.,
10 East 92nd Street, New York, New York 10128.

Library of Congress Cataloging-in-Publication Data
Craig, Theresa.
Edith Wharton : a house full of rooms, architecture, interiors, and gardens / Theresa Craig ; special photography by
John Bessler.
p. cm.
Includes bibliographical references and index.
ISBN 1-885254-42-3 (hardcover)
1. Wharton, Edith, 1862–1937—Contributions in interior
decoration. 2. Wharton, Edith, 1862–1937—Homes and
haunts. I. Wharton, Edith, 1862–1937. II. Title.
NK2004.3.W47C7 1996
747.213—dc20   96-22036

Printed and bound in Hong Kong
Designed by Abigail Sturges

*Page 1: Detail of plaster medallion in the dining room at
The Mount, Lenox, Massachusetts*

*Page 2: Edith Wharton on the terrace of Ste. Claire, Hyères,
ca. 1920–30*

*Page 5: Frontispiece illustration (by A. B. Wenzell, The
House of Mirth, first edition, 1905*

Page 6: Gardens at Ste. Claire, 1920s–1930s

Page 8: Dining room at The Mount

Page 11: Signature on book cover

*I have sometimes thought
that a woman's nature is like
a great house full of rooms.*

—Edith Wharton,
    "The Fullness of Life," 1891

Acknowledgments

MANY PEOPLE CONTRIBUTE TO THE MAKING OF A BOOK AND THOSE WHO EASED my way in the research and preparation of this one include: Janet L. Anderson; Stanley Barrows, professor emeritus of the Parsons School of Design; Patricia Breinin; Rebecca Cape at the Lilly Library of Indiana University at Bloomington; Anne Cherry; Erin C. Clermont; Trent Duffy; Becky Fite; Marc Glick; Thomas S. Hayes; Victoria Mathews; Gianfranco Monacelli; Andrea Monfried; Patricia McCormack; Scott Marshall, deputy director of Edith Wharton Restoration at The Mount; Lori Misura of the Beinecke Library at Yale University; Michael D. Murphy; Angela Palmisono; Monique Panaggio of the Preservation Society of Newport County; Janet Parks of the Avery Library at Columbia University; Rosemarie Reed; Steve Sears; Abigail Sturges; Ellen Thunder; Marlene Tungseth; Prince Philipp and Princess Isabelle von Liechtenstein; and Patricia Willis of the Beinecke Library at Yale University.

Contents

EDITH WHARTON

A Sense of Place

He ushered her into a slip of a hall hung with old prints. She noticed the letters and notes heaped on the table among his gloves and sticks; then she found herself in a small library, dark but cheerful, with its walls of books, a pleasantly faded Turkey rug, a littered desk, and as he had foretold, a tea-tray on a low table near the window. A breeze had sprung up, swaying inward the muslin curtains and bringing a fresh scent of mignonette and petunias from the flower-box on the balcony.

Lily sank with a sigh into one of the shabby leather chairs.

"How delicious to have a place like this all to one's self! What a miserable thing it is to be a woman." She leaned back in a luxury of discontent.

Selden was rummaging in a cupboard for the cake.

"Even women," he said, "have been known to enjoy the privileges of a flat."

"Oh, governesses or widows. But not girls—not poor, miserable, marriageable girls!"

—Lily Bart and Lawrence Selden, *The House of Mirth*, 1905

A frivolous society can acquire dramatic significance only through what its frivolity destroys. Its tragic implication lies in its power of debasing people and ideals.

—Edith Wharton on *The House of Mirth* in *A Backward Glance*, 1934

Edith Newbold Jones at age five (portrait by Edward May)

THESE TWO PASSAGES FROM EDITH WHARTON'S WORK HIGHLIGHT HER CONCERN and attention to a sense of place. In *The House of Mirth,* one of her early and successful novels, she succinctly describes Lawrence Selden's apartment in its cozy charm and Lily Bart's longing for a home all her own. Lily, whose life is one of genteel poverty, has been brought up to be an ornament to the man she marries and cannot hope to have such a home unless she weds successfully. Although Lily and Selden are perhaps emotionally suited to each other, they cannot marry, as Selden does not have sufficient means. As a result, both of the characters are victims of the "frivolous society" Wharton describes in the novel.

Wharton herself was a member of this "frivolous society," whose hierarchical structure served as the setting for much of her fiction. Her short stories and novels, including *The House of Mirth*, the Pulitzer Prize–winning *The Age of Innocence*, *Ethan Frome*, *The Mother's Recompense*, *Summer*, and *The Children*, are especially interesting for keen attention to detail in her characters' physical surroundings and psychological makeup. Like Balzac, an author Wharton admired, she was able to set a scene lavishly and to make it feature prominently in the conflicts and comparisons of her characters. The settings in her fiction are more than mere backdrops for the action, they are an integral part of it and are often used metaphorically and dramatically, making her work extremely visual and well suited to dramatic presentation in readings, plays, and films, the most recent being the movie versions of *The Children*, *Ethan Frome*, and *The Age of Innocence*.

Wharton's search for a sense of place was an emotional one, a search that lasted throughout her life, encompassed the development of her sense of aesthetics, and was eloquently detailed in her nonfiction as well as in her literary work. As a woman in her country, class, and historical period, this search was often not an easy one, and she suffered many frustrations in finding a "room of her own," in Virginia Woolf's sense. Wharton's ancestry—her family dated back to Revolutionary America—placed her in an awkward position for a woman who was to become one of America's premier novelists. It has only been in the last two decades that her work has been reevaluated and studied in its entirety. Perhaps this resurgence of interest in her writing, with its themes set in the nineteenth and early twentieth centuries and its reminiscences of historical periods dating back to Revolutionary America, is due to the fact that the United States has now passed two centuries as a cultural entity and enjoys a certain historical perspective.

It is always most illuminating to look at the past through the eyes of a talented and discriminating author, especially one as well positioned and knowledgeable as Edith Wharton. Wharton struggled against the prejudices of her social group regarding intellectual women and women as writers. Her society found "making a scene" the worst possible faux pas, and Wharton had an uphill struggle to become the literary anthropologist that she was and to create "scenes" that have given us substantial insight into the culture and relationships of a certain segment of Americans. The "scenes" she created for herself in her own homes and surroundings and for her characters in the settings of her literary works have their basis in the places she lived and visited in her youth and throughout her eventful life.

Wharton's aesthetic and intellectual interests in her surroundings began in her early childhood and were a lifelong occupation. In fact, a painting of Edith Jones at age five by Edward May shows a young girl with glistening red tresses arranging flowers. Wharton's first observations of her surroundings were centered on the Old New York world of her parents. She was born into this milieu on January 24, 1862, and was baptized Edith Newbold Jones at Grace Church, located at Broadway and Eleventh Street in lower Manhattan. She was the third child and only daughter of George Frederic Jones and Lucretia Stevens Rhinelander, established members of New York society. They took their place among the other prominent New York families of mainly Dutch and English ancestry.

Old New York was Edith Wharton's first home and made a lasting impression on her life and her work. She describes Old New York, often the setting for her fiction, in her memoir *A Backward Glance:* "The Fifth Avenue of that day was a placid and uneventful thoroughfare, along which genteel landaus, broughams and victorias, and more countrified vehicles of the 'carry all' and 'surrey type' moved up and down at decent intervals and a decorous pace." This description can be seen as a metaphor for the activities of her parents and their friends and associates who were involved in real estate, banking, and law and did charitable work while leading staid responsible lives symbolized by the major thoroughfare's elegant vehicles and unhurried pace. Those Old New Yorkers traveling on the avenue were not caught up in the hustle and bustle of merchant trade, the flurry of the creative arts, or the scandal of passionate relationships. This atmosphere, though dear to Edith in its emphasis on European culture and social responsibility, would also prove stifling and repressive to her. This conflict is aptly described in *The Age of Innocence,* set chiefly in 1870s New York (although it was written after the devastation of World War I and published in 1920), which describes the era and recognizes that the world order was changing, a fact Wharton viewed in her memoir as not altogether positive:

Book cover detail of the Worth Monument on Broadway (artwork by Edward C. Caswell), Old New York: New Year's Day, *first edition, 1924*

> In my youth, the Americans of the original States, who in moments of crisis still shaped the national point of view, were the heirs of an old tradition of European culture which the country has now totally rejected . . . The compact world of my youth has receded into a past from which it can only be dug up in bits by the assiduous relic-hunter; and its smallest fragments begin to be worth collecting and putting together before the last of those who knew the live structure are swept away with it.

Wharton herself became one of America's most astute literary "relic-hunters" in her fictional descriptions of Old New York, particularly detailed in her novella series *Old New York* (1924). The clash between the positive values of her social group and their narrow horizons and lack of sympathy to those different in any way from the common mores would form the basis for much of her fiction.

Another impression dating from her early childhood was the home of her paternal aunt Elizabeth Schermerhorn Jones in Rhinecliff, New York. This structure, Wyndcliffe, a Norman Gothic mansion on a cliff overlooking the Hudson, frightened the young Edith, who was under four years old at the time. Her aesthetic sensitivity was already developed enough to be offended. As Wharton recalls in *A Backward Glance,* the ugliness of the house at Rhinecliff frightened her: "My visual sensibility must always have

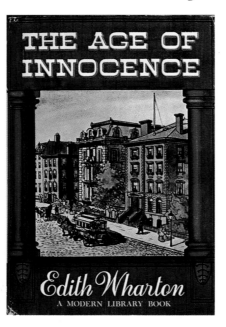

Book jackets, The Age of Innocence, *first edition and 1948 edition*

been too keen for middling pleasures; my photographic memory of rooms and houses—even those seen but briefly, or at long intervals—was from my earliest years a source of inarticulate misery, for I was always vaguely frightened by ugliness." The feeling for beauty, another part of young Edith's imagination, was to remain with her throughout her life and influence her interest in architecture and interior design as well as her appreciation of the natural landscape.

Despite her first impression of her aunt's home, the mansions of the Hudson Valley do figure in her fiction. An example is the Mills Mansion, whose spacious entry hall and drawing room are thought to be the setting of Bellomont, the mansion in which Lily Bart attends a lavish society ball in *The House of Mirth*. Mansions such as the Vanderbilt estate in Hyde Park and the estates of the Livingston family in the Hudson Valley were also part of the circuit of fashionable New York families during the latter part of the nineteenth century.

Europe formed the second set of impressions for young Edith Jones. Due to her father's financial difficulties following the Civil War, Edith's family, except her older brother, Freddy, left for Europe in November 1866 and stayed there for six years. Edith's first year abroad was spent in Rome, where she found beauty in its romantic ruins and sculpture gardens, the Piazza di Spagna, and the flower-strewn hills of the Villa Doria-Pamphili, the Villa

Borghese, and the Palatine. Her youthful love of Italy as well as many subsequent trips there led to the use of Italian settings in Edith's fiction as well as detailed descriptions of the Italian landscape in *Italian Villas and Their Gardens* (1904) and the travel sketches gathered in her volume *Italian Backgrounds* (1905). She also traveled to Spain and visited the Alhambra, Cordova, and Seville, where her impressions were as vivid as those she formed in Rome. She continued to be interested in Spanish themes, and she wrote a series of travel sketches collected in the volume *In Morocco* (1920) about her subsequent visit to that country.

In the winter of 1868, her family moved to Paris for two years. Although Edith's impressions of Paris were not as vivid as those of Rome and Spain, she was impressed by the beauty and style of the Parisians, an impression she used in her fictional descriptions of European characters in French settings. One of young Edith's fond remembrances of her early years in Paris occurs in *A Backward Glance*, where she describes an elegant Parisian: "But all I had eyes for was the lady herself, leaning back as ladies of those days leaned in their indolently-hung carriages, flounces of *feuille-morte* taffetas billowing out about her, and on her rich auburn hair a tiny black lace bonnet with a tea-rose above one ear." Her love and appreciation of French style started early in her life, and along with the intellectual literary enthusiasm of the French, was an important influence on all of her writings as well as on her decision around 1910 to make her home permanently in France.

"*Little Palace of the Garden,*" Parma (pen-and-ink drawing by E. C. Peixoto), Italian Backgrounds

While in Europe, Edith learned to read and discovered her passion for "making up." In her making up Edith recited tales about imaginary characters, whom she describes in *A Backward Glance* as "grown-up people, resembling in appearance and habits my family and their friends, and caught in the same daily coil of 'things that might have happened.'" Here in Edith's early childhood she discovered another passion—the passion for literature—parallel to that of her appreciation of her natural surroundings and aesthetic interiors. She recalled that as a child she was more interested in the creations of her own imagination than in fairy tales.

In 1870 Edith's family was visiting the Black Forest in Germany when the Franco-Prussian War broke out. While in Germany Edith developed typhoid fever and was critically ill, but was fortunately cured. Late in 1870, the family moved to Florence, to an apartment overlooking the Arno. Edith found Florence less pleasant than Rome but continued her studies and delighted in her "making up."

In the summer of 1872, when Edith was ten years old, her family returned to New York. Edith returned with lasting impressions of Italy, France, Spain, and Germany as well as a good command of French, German, and Italian. She also returned with a newfound pleasure in her imaginative stories about the people in her life.

The family returned to New York City and soon went to Pencraig, their home in Newport, Rhode Island, where young Edith was fond of the house and its beautiful natural setting. She recalls in her memoir: "The roomy and pleasant house of Pencraig was surrounded by a verandah wreathed in clematis and honeysuckle, and below it a lawn sloped to a deep daisied meadow, beyond which were a private bathing-beach and boat-landing."

When the family returned to its New York home at 14 West Twenty-third Street, Edith was not impressed by her Old New York surroundings. In *A Backward Glance* she recalls: "One of the most depressing impressions of my childhood is my recollections of the intolerable ugliness of New York, of its untended streets and the narrow houses so lacking in external dignity, so crammed with smug and suffocating upholstery." This lament was concerned with more than the architecture of Old New York, although Edith did seem to be disturbed by the lack of beauty in her external surroundings. Her lament also speaks to the emotional and psychological stuffiness of her parents' world, which in a real sense was suffocating Edith, who suffered throughout her life from asthma and other ailments (which would today be termed psychosomatic). She sought refuge in her father's library and her studies. Edith's brothers were significantly older than she and although her mother was a charming, elegant hostess, she and Edith did not appear to have a very open or close relationship. Lucretia Jones did not share Edith's intellectual interests, although both parents placed great emphasis on proper spoken English. Edith notes in her memoir: "My parents, who were far from intellectual, who read little and studied not at all, nevertheless spoke their mother tongue with scrupulous perfection, and insisted that their children should do the same . . . I have never quite understood how two people so little preoccupied with letters as my father and mother had such sensitive ears for pure English."

Lucretia Jones had Edith show her any novels she wished to read and, following her own upbringing, rejected all the modern novels Edith chose, apparently on the theory that they might be too shocking for a young girl. Edith, however, did not find this too trying, as her mother did allow her to

Edith Newbold Jones in her early twenties

read all the classic novels of world literature, which Edith later felt were perhaps better choices. She also read the principal historians of the time, the English and French poets and dramatists, art history, and art criticism.

Edith was unusual not only in her immediate family but also in her entire social group for her intellectual nature, for her knowledge of Italian, French, and German, and for her desire to use her imagination in writing. There was a certain suspicion of "people who wrote," and many of the contemporary American authors were somewhat suspect, although Washington Irving, Fitz Greene Halleck, and William Dana were acceptable. Herman Melville, a member of the prominent Van Rensselaer family, was excluded for his bohemian tendencies, as was Edgar Allan Poe. Wharton notes in her memoir: "In the eyes of our provincial society authorship was still regarded as something between a black art and a form of manual labour." Apparently she felt that these qualities of authorship made her mother uneasy.

Both of Wharton's parents played a responsible role in their society. The Jones family's wealth came chiefly from real estate, and Frederic Jones managed various investments and served on the board of New York's major charitable organizations, while Lucretia also did charity work but spent most of her time in visiting and entertaining. Edith's parents did attend the theater, not to be stirred by new ideas but to meet and converse with their relatives and friends. Edith was expected to create a life for herself along similar lines and to marry a suitable person. To this end, she made her social debut during the winter season of 1879 in the ballroom of Mrs. Levi Morton on Fifth Avenue near Forty-second Street; she was now an eligible young woman. She spent the summer of 1880 in Bar Harbor, Maine. November 1880 found her leaving for Europe with her family for the sake of her father's health. They moved from London to Cannes to Venice and then back to Cannes early in 1882, where Frederic Jones died, leaving Edith bereft. After her father's death, Edith and her mother returned to Pencraig in Newport; Edith became engaged to Harry Stevens but due primarily to pressure from Harry's family, their engagement was broken off.

It was time for Edith to settle down and she became engaged to the congenial Edward Robbins Wharton of Boston. Teddy, as he was known, showed considerable kindness to Edith and her family during her father's final illness and was of suitable lineage, as the Whartons of Boston were part of the group of families familiar to the social circle of Old New York. To outward appearances Edith and Teddy were well-suited. Perhaps after the death of her father and the lack of an intimate relationship with her mother, the young Edith not only felt the social pressure to marry but was anxious to find her own place in society and to establish a home or space of her own— not a viable option unless she married. Teddy had proven himself kind and dependable, although on many levels he and Edith were mismatched.

Edith Newbold Jones and Edward Robbins Wharton were married on April 29, 1885, at Trinity Chapel, and Lucretia Jones hosted a wedding breakfast for the couple at her new home at 28 West Twenty-fifth Street. Shortly afterward, Edith and Teddy moved into a cottage on the grounds of Pencraig in Newport and lived there from June to February for several years. During each year the couple traveled abroad from February to May. When they were in New York they stayed at the home of Edith's mother.

Edith and Teddy's marriage was not physically fulfilling for either one of them, greatly due to Edith's ignorance of the physical side of marriage, a lack of knowledge she attributed to her mother's inability to enlighten her, although Edith was curious and made inquiries. She and Teddy did try to create a life for themselves at Pencraig Cottage and on their annual European travels, which included a Mediterranean cruise and a trip by horse-drawn carriage from Florence to Urbino with stops at San Marino, San Leo, Loreto, Ancona, Pesaro, and Rimini. They also traveled to Paris, the French Riviera, and Venice.

Edith Newbold Jones in 1890 (portrait by Paillet)

In 1891 Edith acquired a small house on Park Avenue near the corner of Seventy-eighth Street, 884 Park Avenue, and a few years later she bought the house next door, 882 Park Avenue. This home gave her the opportunity to exercise her aesthetic options in the creation of an attractive interior space and to start her life as a more independent woman with her own circle of friends sympathetic to her intellectual nature and pursuits, which Teddy, while he was supportive of her interests, did not share.

In 1893 Edith acquired Land's End in Newport and consulted with the Boston architect and interior designer Ogden Codman Jr. regarding its renovation and furnishing. She also collaborated with Codman on *The Decoration of Houses* (1897), a work on architecture and interior design still consulted by design students and interior designers. This book was Edith's first commercial publication. Although at this time they had two homes in the States, Edith and Teddy traveled widely and made connections and friendships abroad.

Illustration (watercolor by Henry Varnum Poor), Ethan Frome, *1939 edition*

In 1901 Edith bought property in the Berkshires in Lenox, Massachusetts, where she would build a home. Land's End would be sold and Edith hoped to work on the plans for her new home with Ogden Codman. This was not to be, and instead, Edith worked with the New York architect Francis V. L. Hoppin on the plans for The Mount, as her home was called. Edith lavished her attention and funds on The Mount's architecture, interior design, and gardens. There she had a model for the display of her ideas on design and a setting for the furnishings she had purchased abroad. Her love of gardens and keen observation of many European gardens enabled her to create elaborate garden plans for The Mount. Both home and gardens are currently being restored, as they are a testament to Edith Wharton's aesthetic sensibilities and were the scene of some of her fondest memories of productive literary output, including her well-known novel *Ethan Frome,* which uses the area around Lenox as its setting. The Mount was also the scene of stimulating conversations with her friends and literary mentors, including Henry James and Walter Berry, among many others. The building of The Mount coincided with Edith's mother's death but also with her first successful publication of short stories and novels. The Mount became a testament to Wharton's struggle to find a suitable place for herself both physically and psychologically. At The Mount, Edith wrote in her bedroom, which along with her beautifully designed and executed library, certainly provided her with "rooms of her own."

In fact Edith created entire homes and gardens of her own due to her adequate means and passionate interest in and study of architecture and gardens. The Mount was her attempt to carve out her own niche in a social group unsympathetic to, if not suspicious of and puzzled by, her literary concerns. Certainly the resort atmosphere and trivial pursuits of Newport were not conducive to Edith's desire for suitable companionship and a quiet place to write and entertain in a stunning natural environment, both of which The Mount was able to provide.

During the time that Edith owned The Mount, she and Teddy continued their European travels, and Edith established a long-standing connection to the surroundings of English friends and often visited Henry James at his home, Lamb House at Rye in Sussex, and Howard Sturgis at his residence, Queen's Acre, near Windsor. In 1907 the Whartons exchanged their Park Avenue home for an apartment in Paris. They first rented the apartment of the George Vanderbilts at 58, rue de Varenne and later rented their own at 53, rue de Varenne, which Edith occupied until 1920. She found the Faubourg St. Germain extremely congenial and continued her European travels during this period, often taking trips with friends and visiting friends' homes such as the Villa I Tatti, the home of the Bernard Berensons near Florence.

During the faubourg period Edith had a love affair with the American journalist Morton Fullerton. Edith was over forty when she reported experiencing sensual fulfillment for the first time, a fulfillment she considered a beautiful affirmation of the life force. Edith and Teddy's marriage, never really on solid ground, was faltering. Teddy began suffering from serious physical and emotional difficulties and his various love affairs came to light. Teddy and Edith were divorced in 1913.

During the years of World War I, Edith Wharton organized massive relief efforts for French citizens, orphans, and Belgian refugees. She visited the front on several occasions and was awarded the Legion of Honor for her service to France.

Enjoying the Faubourg St. Germain, Edith decided to make her home in France and sold The Mount in 1911. In 1918 she purchased the Pavillon Colombe in St.-Brice-sous-Forêt in the Ile-de-France, a suburb of Paris. Wharton describes her first glimpse of the house through an orchard in *A Backward Glance:* "The orchards were just bursting into bloom, and we seemed to pass through a rosy snow-storm to reach what was soon to be my own door."

Escaping the war and its aftermath in Paris, Edith turned to her new home and recalls in her memoir: "The little house has never failed me since. As soon as I was settled in it peace and order came back into my life. I had leisure for the two pursuits which never palled, writing and gardening and through all the years I have gone on gardening and writing." The purchase and furnishing of the Pavillon Colombe underscore Edith's lifelong search for a sense of place and again signal a break with the social group into which she was born. She considered the European way of life vastly more supportive to her literary pursuits, and she felt that being an author made her acceptable and interesting in French society as opposed to the oddity that she often felt herself to be in her own country.

In 1919 Wharton took a long lease on a property, a former convent, on the Riviera in Hyères. She used Ste. Claire du Vieux Château as a winter residence. Ste. Claire was on a hill, and its rough brick tower peered down on the Mediterranean. In her later years Wharton looked to the tranquil beauty of the Pavillon Colombe and the restorative power of the sun and sea at Ste. Claire to soothe her after the devastation of World War I and to allow her to continue visiting with friends and writing. She built a new, sunny library conducive to reading and musing at Ste. Claire. Often, groups of writers and artists rested on the villa's extensive stone terrace or picnicked in the surrounding countryside. Her last days at the Pavillon Colombe were serene ones and she died there on August 11, 1937. She is buried near Walter Berry at the Cimetière des Gonards near Versailles, in a simple grave in a peaceful place.

Edith Wharton's search for a sense of place took many forms. Her appreciation of natural beauty, classical architecture, elegant furnishings, and restorative gardens drove her to create harmonious homes suited to the needs of their occupants and guests. Her understanding of the need for a home in both the physical and emotional sense enabled her to marshal her considerable forces to the aid of war refugees during World War I. Her lifelong struggle to seek out her own place among companions who understood her intellectual nature and her search for enlightenment on many subjects compelled her constantly to search for intellectual stimulus through her readings and extensive travel. Her feelings of frustration in the stifling air of her class and country's circumscribed roles for women (and men) fired her literary imagination. Her lifelong conflicts and search for knowledge formed the basis of her novels most admired for their style and symmetry and for their almost anthropological or sociological description of the historical triumphs and tragedies of a segment of American culture. Wharton succeeded at being an "assiduous relic-hunter," and her success has afforded her readers considerable pleasure and insight.

THE MOUNT

EDITH WHARTON RESIDENCE
LENOX, MASSACHUSETTS

LENOX, MA
SEP
5
P M
1980
01240

NEW HAVEN, CT
SEP
5
1980
06510

Edith Wharton
USA 15c

Edith Wharton
USA 15c

FIRST DAY OF ISSUE

Charles Scribner's
Sons
New York
1897

The
Decoration of
Houses

By

Edith Wharton
and
Ogden Codman Jr.

The Principles of Design

EDITH WHARTON IS ARGUABLY THE ONLY AMERICAN AUTHOR TO HAVE STUDIED architecture, interior design, and garden planning systematically, and her concern for these subjects, shown particularly in her books *The Decoration of Houses* (1897), written with the architect Ogden Codman Jr., and *Italian Villas and Their Gardens* (1904), is a concern also apparent in her literary work, travel writings, and letters. Wharton's setting of aesthetic scenes is the trademark of her novels as well as of her homes and gardens. Just as she collaborated with architects sympathetic to her principles of design, such as Codman and Francis V. L. Hoppin, in the plans for her homes, she and her publishers also worked with noted artists such as Maxfield Parrish and book designers such as Berkeley Updike, who added an important aesthetic dimension to her literary works. The result of these collaborations was a symmetrical blending of form and content, a synthesis that occupied Wharton throughout her life.

Title page, The Decoration of Houses, *first edition, 1897*

THE DECORATION OF HOUSES

Ogden Codman Jr. worked with Edith and Teddy Wharton on the refurbishing of their Newport home, Land's End, and in late 1895 started collaborating with Edith on *The Decoration of Houses*. Codman was raised in France and was primarily interested in French classical architecture. His most noted work was in interior design, although he was the principal architect on over twenty houses. In addition to interior design for several of Edith's homes, he decorated ten bedrooms at the Breakers, Cornelius Vanderbilt's mansion in Newport, and furnished Kykuit, John D. Rockefeller Jr.'s house in North Tarrytown, New York.

Vanderbilt Mansion,
Hyde Park, New York

Along with Codman's interest in classical styles, Wharton was also impressed by Charles McKim and Stanford White, architects who took American architecture and interior decoration into the twentieth century, and who pioneered a close working relationship between architects and interior designers. In fact Wharton has been closely associated with the birth of interior design in the United States. Edward Lucie-Smith writes in *Furniture*, "It has been said that the person who invented the concept of interior decoration as we know it today was the novelist Edith Wharton . . . She preached a cautious, sensible good taste, albeit on rather a grand scale, which has been the stock-in-trade of most professional decorators ever since."

The introduction to *Decoration of Houses* demonstrates this "sensible good taste." Wharton and Codman felt that in the late 1820s architecture and interior design became separated and as a result interior design became merely decoration with little regard for the feeling of the house as a whole. The authors were encouraged by the development of a new relationship between accomplished designers and architects: "Now, in the hands of deco-

The entrance hall of the
Vanderbilt Mansion

rators who understand the fundamental principles of their art, the surest effects are produced, not at the expense of simplicity and common sense, but by observing the requirements of both. These requirements are identical with those regulating domestic architecture, the chief end in both cases being the suitable accommodation of the inmates of the house." The historical models for modern architecture are those styles "prevailing in Italy since 1500, in France from the time of Louis XIV, and in England since the introduction of the Italian manner by Inigo Jones."

Wharton and Codman continue giving practical advice in their overall discussion of rooms. The first consideration in interior decoration is the purpose of each individual room; rooms designed to serve several functions are probably not ideal. The tastes and activities of the occupants of the home should dictate the decoration of the rooms. A study of the house plan, including all elevations, and of any detailed architectural renderings should be made before the process of room decoration begins. Proportion leading to harmony is the key principle of interior decoration, and "In deciding upon a scheme of decoration, it is necessary to keep in mind the relation of furniture to ornament, and of the room as a whole to other rooms in the house." Start with clear architectural principles in each room and use the most tasteful furniture available rather than mixing fine pieces with less desirable ones. The purchase of new furniture, if this is possible, should be decided on after consultation with the decorator, as "neither decoration nor furniture, however good of its kind, can look its best unless each is chosen with reference to the other."

Since designing a room is a combination of architecture, furniture, and decoration, it is important that the architect and decorator have similar training, so that a harmonious result will be achieved. To achieve this harmony the authors recommend the architectural styles of the historic models they favor, plain furniture of fine wood in the style of French and English eighteenth-century artisans, and tasteful, simple decorative elements.

*Mills Mansion, Staatsburg,
New York*

The important elements of a room are walls, doors, windows, fireplaces, ceilings, and floors. The purpose of walls requires careful consideration. Wall treatments will differ if the walls are to be used as a background for paintings, for example, or if the walls themselves will be the major decoration of the room. Doors should be viewed in relation to their importance in the house, with the chief door having the most elaborate treatment. Doors should generally remain closed in the interests of the purpose of the room and the inhabitants' privacy, and should always open into a room to make entering simple and to make the room inviting. Windows enjoy a primary place in room decoration: "Not only do they represent the three chief essentials of its comfort,—light, heat and means of access,—but they are the leading features in that combination of voids and masses that forms the basis of architectural harmony." The fireplace was the focal point of the room in the historical models taken as examples of fine architecture, and a beautifully designed fireplace, ranging from the elaborate to the simple, serves the same aesthetic function in the twentieth century. A room's ceiling is more important in creating an overall impression than its decoration. Just as in wall decoration, ceiling decoration should be harmonious, and one part of the ceiling decoration should be chosen as a focal point. In the same manner as walls and ceilings, floors serve as backdrops for the decoration of the room and should be somewhat unobtrusive.

The final elements in room decoration are small decorative objects, or bric-a-brac. There are two types of decorative ornaments: objects of art such as paintings or statues and useful object such as lamps, clocks, and fire screens. It is best to seek out the most tasteful decorative objects and arrange them harmoniously among the furniture of a room. If a room is too cluttered, even with numerous tasteful objects, the result will detract from the aesthetic values of the objects themselves and from the symmetry of the room as a whole. The details of even small decorative-object placement are not so trivial that they should not be given due consideration, as "A room should depend for its adornment on general harmony of parts, and on the artistic quality of such necessities as lamps, screens, bindings, and furniture. Whoever goes beyond these essentials should limit himself in the choice of ornaments to the 'labors of the master-artist's hand.'"

The Decoration of Houses gives practical advice on the various categories of rooms in a home, advice devoted to the clear purpose of each room and to its architectural design and decoration. The types of rooms reviewed are entrance and vestibule; hall and stairs; drawing room, boudoir, and morning room; ballroom, salon ("saloon" in *Decoration of Houses*), music room, and gallery; library, smoking room, and den; dining room; bedrooms; and schoolroom and nurseries. The rooms described are rather lavish, but the principles of harmony and proportion can be adapted to less elaborate rooms.

The front hall of the Mills Mansion ca. 1900

Each room must be suited to the house as a whole, so that a vestibule may range from the informal setting of a country cottage to the elegant setting of a townhouse. Entrances both admit and exclude and should appear up to both tasks. The door should be sturdy, weather resistant, and secure, and the simple furnishings of the vestibule should also be sturdy and able to withstand the comings and goings of a busy household without needing numerous minor repairs. The vestibule requires a door opening onto the street and another opening onto an inner hall.

The staircase should be close to the vestibule but not necessarily in the same room, as the staircase is generally used only by the inhabitants of the house, while the vestibule may be used by many others. It is preferable for the vestibule to open onto a hall that leads to the staircase. The rooms closest to the outdoors are more formal in nature. Therefore the vestibule is the most formal room of this group, with the hall a bit less formal and of a

The blue bedroom of the Vanderbilt Mansion; the breakfast room of the Breakers, Newport, Rhode Island

slightly more colorful design, and the living rooms the most informal and intimate. The furniture of the hall should consist of simple tables and benches or chairs. The walls and stair railing of a staircase should be stone or marble, and carpeting of the stairs should be in a uniform color. Heavily designed treatments of the walls of a staircase, such as wallpaper or fabric hangings, should be avoided. If paintings or prints are hung on the walls of the hall, their subjects should not be too complex as they will be viewed only in passing.

The history of the early-twentieth-century drawing room encompasses two earlier models, that of the *salon de famille*, or family living room, and the *salon de compagnie*, a festively decorated room reserved for entertaining. The *salon de compagnie* is not necessary in an average home and will probably not be used very often, as is the case with an exceedingly formal *salon de famille*. A comfortable, inviting *salon de famille* is, however, very much a necessity. If the house is grand enough to accommodate a *salon de compagnie*, it should be tastefully but sparsely furnished, as it may accommodate quite a number of guests. The walls should be colorfully decorated in a light hue. Paintings and small works of art cannot be properly appreciated in a festive setting where many people gather for short periods of time; such works are more appropriate in the *salon de famille*, where the family may spend many hours. The living room would ideally contain eighteenth-century French furniture or reproductions of the standard armchair (bergère), desks, and tables of various sizes, and one or more tastefully designed bookcases containing artistically bound volumes on sympathetic subjects.

The boudoir is actually part of a bedroom suite, but in the twentieth-century home, a sitting room off the *salon de famille* may become the boudoir for the mistress of the house and may be furnished with a lounge chair modeled on the French *lit de repos*, a writing desk for organizing household affairs, and other small-scale tables, chairs, and lamps. Small paintings and objects of art that would be lost in a larger room may be displayed here to good advantage.

The morning room may serve as an informal version of the *salon de famille*, if the family room contains the best furniture and decorative objects. The English morning room served as a place for the family to gather in casual sporting attire that may have been wet or muddy after outdoor activities. The appointments of the morning room should be sturdy and as easy to maintain as possible.

The ballroom, salon, music room, and gallery are considered gala rooms and may not be found in the average home. If the house is large enough to include these rooms, they should be used only for their intended

The boudoir at the Pavillon Colombe, probably in the 1920s

purpose: entertaining a large number of guests. The salon is typically a high-ceilinged room—it can be two stories—with dramatic wall decoration and architectural elements opening to a gallery or galleries reached by concealed staircases. There are modest and elaborate versions of this combination of rooms. A gallery may overhang the salon or be adjacent to it. The gallery may be a longish room used to display the art collection of the home's owners or may be used as a salon or ballroom.

Ballrooms also run the gamut from modest to lavish, but there are several applicable general principles. Since ballrooms should be relatively free of furniture, the wall and ceiling treatments provide the decorative elements. These treatments can be architectural as well as decorative. Ballrooms may have multicolored marble columns and statues, frescoed ceilings and walls, mirrored wall paneling, or sumptuous tapestries. Ballrooms should be lit from the ceiling with soft light from chandeliers and should have tasteful benches along the walls.

The music room is not necessarily reserved exclusively for entertaining large crowds but is somewhat different in function from the rooms in daily use. It may be suitable when entertaining small groups of guests. Acoustics must be considered in decorating the music room; heavy curtains and fabric hangings must be avoided as they can muffle sound, whereas a domed ceiling, if possible, might improve the room's acoustics. The music room should have an atmosphere of tranquillity and spaciousness.

*The library at
The Mount
ca. 1900–1910*

In the library, beautifully crafted books as works of art can be arranged in aesthetically pleasing yet practical arrangements. Built-in bookcases, for example, both make the bookcases part of the decoration of the walls and make the volumes accessible to the reader. Books themselves should be the focal point of a library; other ornaments should be used with moderation. Tables should be quite large so that a number of books and publications may be comfortably accommodated, and a sturdy chair should complement the table. The arrangement of libraries, certainly an important concern for Edith Wharton, shows her aptitude for a successful blend of form and content.

A small smoking room or den for the master of the house can be made comfortable despite space constraints. The den may be a smallish room on the first floor of the home. It can be made to appear more spacious by the use of light-colored paneled walls with a plain or simply decorated ceiling.

An easy chair and a well-constructed table that can accommodate books and a lamp are the only absolutely necessary furnishings.

In the family dining room, matters of taste and practicality are paramount. If the windows have a good architectural treatment, draperies are not necessary. A stone or marble floor is preferable, and if carpets are used they should not be fixed to the floor. Lighting should be from overhead chandeliers or wall sconces. The walls are often paneled in light-colored wood or feature murals of flowers or fruit or *nature morte* paintings. A round or square table with tapering legs is preferable to the English-style rectangular extension table. Few homes are grand enough to require state or banquet rooms, and in the houses where they exist, this type of room is considered a gala room and is decorated in the style of other gala rooms. If a house contains a banquet hall, it probably also contains what has been called a breakfast room, which corresponds in decoration to the family dining room.

The genesis of the twentieth-century bedroom owes much to French eighteenth-century design as well as to the introduction of cotton fabric. When the bedroom was utilized as a salon—a custom that persisted into the eighteenth century—the lady of the house would receive important visitors while lying in bed. As a result, considerable craftsmanship went into the design and creation of lavishly ornate bedsteads. Cotton fabrics of interesting design had been imported from India, and in the latter half of the eighteenth century French design and manufacture of cotton fabric began. French designers were influenced by Chinese pattern design but added fanciful elements to their own schemes. The availability of washable curtains, slipcovers, and bed linens in attractive designs lent variety to the French bedroom, as the rooms' fabric furnishings could be varied with the seasons.

Period photograph of Gertrude Vanderbilt Whitney's bedroom at the Breakers

The bedroom suite, composed of several small rooms, is a French contribution to room arrangement. Wharton and Codman write: "Where space is not restricted there should, in fact, be four rooms, preceded by an antechamber separating the suite from the main corridor of the house. The small sitting-room or boudoir opens into this antechamber; and next comes the bedroom, beyond which are the dressing and bath rooms." This plan is only used in quite large houses, but if space is not a consideration, the bedroom suite is an interesting option. When bedrooms ceased to function as salons, their design and decoration became less ornate. Heavy draperies and upholstery are not necessary to the function of the room or beneficial to the health of the inhabitants. The bedroom proper should be furnished with only the bedstead and its accessories, while the boudoir may have a writing table, a *lit de repos,* and an armchair or two. The dressing-room furnishings consist of a dressing table, washstand, and an eighteenth-century-style clothes-press and chiffoniers. The bathroom, as any other room, should have a harmonious architectural treatment with marble or tile waterproof walls and floor.

In the early part of the twentieth century privileged children were educated at home and required a schoolroom as well as a nursery. Schoolrooms should be aesthetically pleasing, which will make them more congenial to the pursuits of study and appreciation of beauty. Children might well appreciate art prints or reproductions of sculpture as well as artistically crafted books. Avoid dark colors and use white woodwork and vibrant colors on the walls, which should be decorated with tasteful representations of the subjects of study, which may be changed often for study and variety. The schoolroom should be equipped with a substantial writing table and a bookcase with glass doors.

Nurseries and children's rooms should have hardwood floors with removable carpets and painted walls decorated with tasteful colored prints. Windows require either curtains or shades. Children should be able to choose the wall decorations for their rooms. Edith Wharton almost comments on her own childhood aesthetic sensibilities in this passage: "The child's visible surroundings form the basis of the best, because of the most unconscious, cultivation: and not of aesthetic cultivation only, since, as has been pointed out, the development of any artistic taste, if the child's general training is of the right sort, indirectly broadens the whole view of life." Form and content are once again blended in this conception of aesthetic sensibility.

ITALIAN VILLAS AND THEIR GARDENS

Wharton wrote a series of articles for *Century* magazine on the villas and gardens of Italy, which were published in book form by the Century company in 1904. The book was illustrated with detailed, atmospheric watercolors by the noted illustrator Maxfield Parrish, although Wharton had told her publisher that she preferred garden plans. Fortunately Parrish's exquisite watercolors did appear in the first edition. The volume was reissued in paperback in 1988, a testament to its lasting value. In an introductory essay to the most recent edition, Henry Hope Reed discusses the lasting nature of both of Wharton's writings on architectural subjects:

Her first commercial publication—*The Decoration of Houses* (1897), written with Ogden Codman, Jr.—was and remains the best book, by far, on the subject. Taking a place next to *Decoration* is *Italian Villas and Their Gardens*, published in 1904 . . . Edith Wharton stands as one of the outstanding figures of her generation along with certain painters, sculptors, and architects who seized on the great classical tradition of Western art and used it to help shape the arts of our country.

The World's Columbian Exposition of 1893 in Chicago was a showcase for the rebirth of interest in the Western classical tradition in architecture and garden design in the United States. Examples of this tradition intimately known to Wharton were the Vanderbilt homes in New York City, the Hudson Valley, and Newport, and the decorative architecture springing up in New York City, such as the erection of civic buildings and monuments in the classical tradition, the decoration of building facades, the overall plans of Grand Central Station and Pennsylvania Station, the Metropolitan Museum, and the main branch of the public library.

Grand Central Station in 1875

Public parks and private gardens also benefited from this resurgence in interest in classical garden design, as demonstrated by the landscape design of both Central Park and Prospect Park by Frederick Law Olmsted and Calvert Vaux. Stanford White, an architect who very much interested Wharton, designed classical ornaments for Prospect Park. Private estates added gardens in cities along the eastern seaboard and northern California, among other locations. Frederick Law Olmsted planned formal gardens for George Washington Vanderbilt's home Biltmore in Asheville, North Carolina, and Ogden Codman Jr. planned a formal garden for the Grange in Lincoln, Massachusetts. These grand estates employed European-trained gardeners, as a taste for scientific garden maintenance became apparent. In 1900 Central Park built a conservatory and the New York Botanical Garden in the Bronx opened. In 1901 the Horticultural Society of New York was founded. In the early part of the twentieth century, a number of women landscape architects with an interest in floriculture became prominent. Among this group were Annette Flanders, Marion Cruger Coffin, Ellen Shipman, and Edith Wharton's niece Beatrix Jones Farrand. Farrand designed the Dumbarton Oaks gardens in Washington, D.C., and the Rockefeller gardens on Mount Desert Island, Maine, and assisted Wharton in planning her gardens at The Mount in Lenox. Farrand was the only woman founding member of the American Society of

Landscape Architects; included in her more public projects were the landscape designs of the Yale and Princeton campuses.

Against this background of American interest in classical garden design, Edith Wharton produced her own study in *Italian Villas and Their Gardens*. In "Italian Magic," the aptly titled introduction to her volume, she discusses the overall structure and harmonious elements in garden design. Wharton felt that since flowers are subject to changing and harsh weather conditions, they should be subsidiary elements in garden planning, although her own gardens show a taste for carefully chosen flowers. The three primary garden elements are marble, water, and "perennial verdure." The elements of the garden are to blend harmoniously with the architecture of the villa as well as with the natural landscape. The garden design of the Renaissance was the chief model Wharton observed in the villas she visited. Her study includes villas in and near Rome, Florence, Siena, Genoa, Lombardy, and Venice. Wharton brings our attention to two types of villas identified by the Italian architects of earlier centuries: "the *villa suburbana,* or *maison de plaisance* (literally the pleasure-house), standing within or just without the city walls, surrounded by pleasure-grounds and built for a few weeks' residence; and the country house, which is an expansion of the old farm, and stands generally farther out of town, among its fields and vineyards—the seat of the country gentleman living on his estates." The type of villa dictates the type of garden to be planned, just as modern gardens must be planned in harmonious relationship to their houses. Although there were rich French and English garden traditions, Wharton favored the Italian garden style as more closely related to the Renaissance period she found so congenial. As Arthur Ross succinctly writes in his foreword to *Italian Villas:* "Italian style, more orderly than the loosely organized English Romantic landscape, and less rigidly formal than the French, reaffirms the unique and lasting architectural inspiration of the Renaissance period."

The secret of Italian Renaissance "garden-magic" resided for Wharton in the adaptation of garden to villa and nature. In the example of the hill towns of Italy, the hillside would feature prominently in any architectural plan as well as in the architecture of the villa and the needs of the villa's inhabitants. When these concerns are satisfied, the requirements of specific garden plans can be approached:

> The inherent beauty of the garden lies in the grouping of its parts—in the converging lines of its long ilex-walks, the alteration of sunny open spaces with cool woodland shade, the proportion between terrace and bowling-green, or between the height of a wall and the width of a path. None of these details was negligible to the landscape architect of the Renaissance: he considered the distribution of shade and

Book cover, Italian Villas and Their Gardens, *first edition, 1904; illustrations (by Maxfield Parrish) of a garden area at the Villa Gamberaia, near Florence, and the Boboli Gardens, Rome, from* Italian Villas and Their Gardens

sunlight, of straight lines of masonry and rippled lines of foliage, as carefully as he weighed the relation of his whole composition to the scene about it.

To this end Wharton offered advice to her contemporary gardeners. Gardens have much in common with homes. A substantial garden can be divided into "rooms" according to their purposes. The passageways in gardens should be wide enough for comfortable access from one part to another, and shaded for protection in summer while sunny and sheltered for protection in winter. Garden "rooms" can range from secluded areas with enclosing foliage to a wide expanse of lawn or flower beds, to paths studded with marble statues or overhung with vines, to walled cloisters with soothing fountains. Wharton offers Italian villas as examples of these myriad possibilities.

The primary design principles of harmony and proportion are much in evidence in both *The Decoration of Houses* and *Italian Villas and Their Gardens.* They are equally present in Edith Wharton's aesthetic choices, from the overall architectural plans for The Mount to her attention to detail in the well-chosen, well-placed decorative object.

BOBOLI

GAMBERAIA

First Impressions
1862–1885

AFTER THE JONES FAMILY'S 1866–72 SOJOURN IN EUROPE, EDITH WAS INTRODUCED to her American surroundings. These surroundings centered on fashionable post–Civil War New York, the stately mansion-villas of the Hudson Valley, and the summer resort homes of Newport, Rhode Island. Edith observed first-hand in these locations the work of America's most prominent artists, architects, interior designers, and landscape gardeners. These first American impressions affected the creation of her fiction as well as the creation of her homes. Wharton often returned to these settings in her most accomplished works. *The House of Mirth* has scenes set in Old New York and the Hudson Valley. Her novella series *Old New York* has stories set in the 1840s, 1850s, 1860s, and 1870s. *The Age of Innocence* has scenes in Old New York and fashionable Newport in the 1870s. *Hudson River Bracketed* and *The Gods Arrive* are partially set in the Hudson Valley. Not surprisingly, some of the actual places known to the young Edith Newbold Jones appear in thinly disguised form in her fiction.

Illustrations (by Edward C. Caswell) of Gramercy Park, Old New York: The Old Maid, and of an interior, Old New York: The Spark

OLD NEW YORK

The New York of Edith Jones' family and friends included lower Fifth Avenue, Gramercy Park, Union Square Park, Madison Square, and Washington Park. It extended north on Fifth Avenue past St. Patrick's Cathedral, completed in 1879 (and strangely reminiscent of Ste. Clothilde's in Paris, the church nearest to Edith's future Paris apartment). The northern boundary of Old New York was the Metropolitan Museum of Art.

From 1872 to 1880, when her family returned to Europe due to her father's ill health, Edith had the opportunity to compare her impressions of New York with her impressions of Europe. Steeped in classical architecture from early childhood, she found brownstone New York at first uniformly ugly. Her family's home at 14 West Twenty-third Street was a three-story brownstone, a residence not in keeping with the principles of decoration she later espoused in *The Decoration of Houses*. R. W. B. Lewis describes it in *Edith Wharton:*

> Passing up the inevitable Dutch stoop, one entered a vestibule painted in Pompeian red, and beyond it the first of several cramped sitting rooms. The white-and-gold drawing room on the second floor was rigorously protected from the world outside by two layers of curtains: sashes, lace draperies, and damask hangings. Heavy pieces of Dutch marquetry adorned it and a cabinet displayed a number of old painted fans and exquisite and never-used pieces of old lace brought back from Venice and Paris. A Mary Magdalene, etched in copper, was on the Louis Philippe table: in the dining room, adjoining, there was an imitation Domenichino; both were nearly invisible in the well-bred gloom.

This home was narrow and would appear overcrowded, with its rooms by necessity having to serve more than one function, a situation Wharton was strongly to counsel against in architectural and decorating schemes. Nevertheless, George Frederic and Lucretia Jones entertained regularly and attended the theater and the opera. Lucretia was a hostess well respected for the quality of her food and the guests at her parties. These guests came from a circumscribed list of families known to each other, and their conversation centered on family plans and visits, the upkeep of their various summer homes, and European travel plans. Very rarely did the conversation turn to cultural topics such as the latest concert or art exhibit. These events were generally occasions for social intercourse rather than for evaluation of the entertainment or artwork at hand.

Edith's life at this juncture comprised lessons with her tutor Anna Bahlmann, nurturing by Hannah Doyle, her nanny, and visits to Gramercy Park with her friend Emelyn Washburn, the daughter of the rector of Calvary Church. Edith's happiest moments might have been spent in her father's library where she regarded his books as exciting treasures. As she recalls in *A Backward Glance:*

> I have wandered far from my father's library. Though it had the leading share in my growth I have let myself be drawn from it by one scene after another of my parents' life in New York or on their travels. But the library calls me back, and I pause on its threshold, averting my eyes from the monstrous oak mantel supported on the heads of vizored knights, and looking past them at the rows of handsome bindings and familiar names.

The exterior (partially shown at right ca. 1875) and interior (ca. 1884) of the Jones family home at 14 West Twenty-third Street; West Twenty-third Street between Fifth and Sixth Avenues in 1898, slightly west of the Jones house

Old New York: New
Year's Day gathering,
1868; strollers in
Madison Square, 1889;
Madison Square Garden
colonnade, 1891;
skating in Central
Park, 1877; Century
Club (designed by
Stanford White), 1889

*Wyndcliffe, Rhinecliff,
New York: south facade,
view of the Hudson River
from the grounds, foliage-
covered stairs to main door*

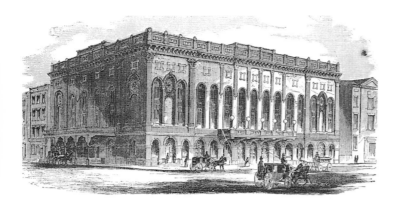

Old New York:
exterior and interior of
the Academy of Music
at Fourteenth Street and
Irving Place, 1856

The young Edith wrote her first poems and stories in this library. In 1878 Lucretia had a selection of Edith's poems privately published in Newport.

Edith Jones made her social debut in late 1879 in a private ballroom belonging to Mrs. Levi Morton on Fifth Avenue near Forty-second Street. After this ritual, Edith enjoyed many of the activities common to her social set. There were elegant lengthy parties and after-dinner calls. Young women did not attend universities but spent this period before marriage preparing for their future roles as wives and mothers. Edith was so fascinated by knowledge and literary pursuits that she must have found it exceedingly difficult to stifle such leanings in the interest of social decorum.

For the young men and women of Edith's fashionable set, the social "season" was the winter. Festivities began in early December and included gala balls at Delmonico's or Mrs. Astor's ballroom at Fifth Avenue and Thirty-fourth Street. Outdoor activities included tobogganing, sleigh riding, and ice skating in Central Park. The young people often met at lunch parties

Charity ball at the Metropolitan Opera House, 1884; Vanderbilt Mansion, Fifth Avenue

and receptions. The Union and Century Clubs provided locations for the pursuits of the young men. Like their parents, the younger groups attended theater performances at the Stanford White–designed Madison Square Garden as well as the Academy of Music at Fourteenth Street and Irving Place. The new crop of wealthy New Yorkers was denied boxes at the Academy by the old guard and decided to build their own opera house on Broadway between Thirty-ninth and Fortieth Streets. The opening of their new house, the Metropolitan Opera House, took place in October 1883 with a performance of *Faust* with the soprano Christine Nilsson as Marguerite. It is this very opera that is portrayed in the opening pages of *The Age of Innocence*.

Fashionable families began to move uptown from the residences and public spaces of lower Fifth Avenue, birthplace of Old New York society, and well-designed buildings were constructed, including Pennsylvania Station, Grand Central Station, the Vanderbilt Mansion on Fifth Avenue between Fifty-first and Fifty-second Streets, and the Metropolitan Museum

*Wyndcliffe: arched
ceiling, wooden
staircase*

of Art. Edith's relative Mary Mason Jones, on whom the character Mrs. Manson Mingott is based in *The Age of Innocence,* lived in an elegant home on Fifth Avenue in the fifties, an area of town thought to be quite far from the hub of activities centered on the residences and social activities of lower Fifth Avenue. The young Edith often borrowed books from the Society Library, as the Astor Library was called. Located in an Italianate building on Lafayette Place (now Lafayette Street), this library was constructed with a bequest from John Jacob Astor and was built in stages following the designs of the architects Alexander Saeltzer, Griffith Thomas, and Thomas Stent. In

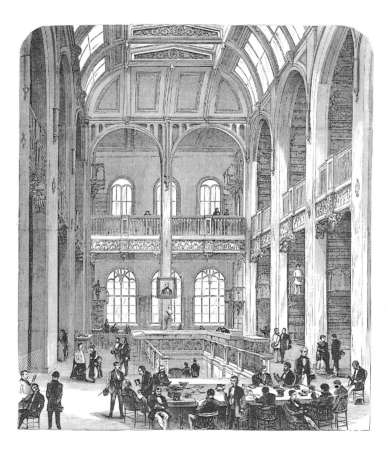

The Astor Library, 1875

1912 the collections of the Astor Library, the Lenox Library, and the Tilden Foundation were merged to start the main branch of the New York Public Library on Fifth Avenue and Forty-second Street.

Upon her return from Europe after her father's death in 1882, Edith had another opportunity to view architectural and decorating developments in Old New York. After their marriage in 1885 she and Teddy regularly spent time in New York, residing at the new home of Lucretia Jones at 28 West Twenty-fifth Street before they acquired a New York house.

The architectural styles Edith observed and admired during this period corresponded to the decorative methods she later explored in *The Decoration of Houses.* The taste for a more classical approach in American architecture was not shared by all the country's architects or homeowners but was by the architects Edith favored. She understood and appreciated the work of the firm McKim, Mead & White; Ogden Codman Jr.; and Richard Morris Hunt, among others. Chicago's World's Columbian Exposition of 1893 had several pavilions demonstrating the beauty of Renaissance architecture. The Administration Building was designed by Richard Morris Hunt, the first American to attend the Ecole des Beaux-Arts in Paris, and the Agricultural Building by McKim, Mead & White. In fact, all the buildings for the exposition were inspired by the architecture of the Renaissance, in particular by the type of cornices used first in Florence and then throughout Italy. As David Garrard Lowe writes in *Stanford White's New York:* "These powerful projections served to control the streetscape and directed the eye of the viewer to some prearranged physical or psychological vanishing point. It was the uniformly mandated cornice line which gave to

Chicago's 1893 Fair its sense of harmony and unity though the buildings were by a multitude of architects."

The influence that certain architects had on Wharton can be seen in concrete ways. In *The House of Mirth* she names Lawrence Selden's apartment building the Benedick after a bachelor apartment building called the Benedict, where Stanford White did a bit of socializing in the 1880s. In *Stanford White's New York,* Lowe writes: "In the middle 1880s much of White's social life centered on the apartment building for bachelors, the Benedict, which McKim, Mead & Bigelow had designed in 1879 on the east side of Washington Square." Stanford White also designed the Church of the Ascension on lower Fifth Avenue and worked with the artists Augustus Saint-Gaudens and David Maitland Armstrong on its decoration. The church was a tribute to the architecture and decorative arts of the Renaissance. Charles McKim worked on the chancel, and Lowe reports that McKim was thinking of the chancel's French walnut pulpit when he wrote to Wharton: "By conscientious study of the best examples of classic periods, it is possible to conceive a perfect result."

Another direct relation with Wharton was Stanford White's choice for the interior decorator of the women's Colony Club, which he designed. He selected the former actress Elsie de Wolfe, who had redecorated her small townhouse on Irving Place near Seventeenth Street according to the principles of *The Decoration of Houses,* which she had read and admired. White felt that he and de Wolfe had similar tastes and concerns and that their collaboration would be a sympathetic one. Wharton then was not only influenced by the architecture and decorative arts of Old New York but had her own subtle effect on their evolution.

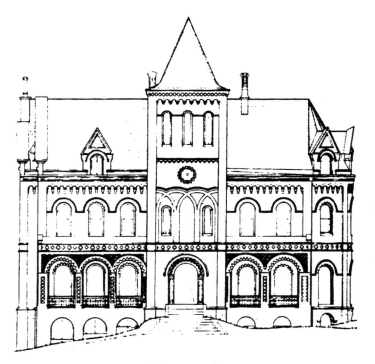

South elevation of Wyndcliffe (drawn in 1974)

MANSIONS OF THE HUDSON VALLEY

Three Hudson Valley villas that made an impression on the young Edith were Wyndcliffe in Rhinecliff, the Vanderbilt Mansion in Hyde Park, and the Mills Mansion in Staatsburg. These elaborate homes figured in her imagination as well as in her fiction.

Wyndcliffe belonged to Edith's aunt, Elizabeth Schermerhorn Jones, a cousin of Mrs. William Astor. It was constructed in 1853 on an eighty-acre

Vanderbilt Mansion, Hyde Park, New York: main facade, garden pavilion, gardens

estate called Linden Grove under the direction of an architect named Gardiner of Boston and using the work of a builder and master mason from New York City. The home was a twenty-four-room turreted summer villa. It is currently almost in ruins, but it still has the power to evoke the days of its former glory. Scenic views of the Hudson and the Catskill Mountains can be seen from its four-story central tower. Wyndcliffe has a brick facade with walls and turrets of elaborate brickwork. The brickwork contains designs of crosses, diamonds, triangles, and squares around the decorative arches and lancet windows. The interior also boasts vaulted ceilings and beautifully crafted and designed wooden stairways, whose remnants are still visible. There are also the remains of decorative fireplace mantels and chandeliers. Originally the estate extended from the mansion's site on a hillside to within one-half mile of the river, and guests could enjoy a game of tennis on the lawn courts. Wyndcliffe is certainly an impressive ruin and in its day was termed "a very successful house with much the appearance of some of the smaller Scotch castles" by Henry Winthrop Sargent, owner of the Hudson Valley villa Wodenethe.

Edith visited Wyndcliffe when she was very young, primarily under the age of four, and for her the mansion was terrifying. As she recalls in *A Backward Glance:* "The effect of terror produced by the house of Rhinecliff was no doubt due to what seemed to me its intolerable ugliness . . . I can still remember hating everything at Rhinecliff, which, as I saw, on rediscovering it some years later, was an expensive but dour specimen of Hudson River Gothic." Even with this first impression, Wharton gave Wyndcliffe a somewhat more sympathetic treatment in her novel *Hudson River Bracketed,* where it serves as a disguised model for the Willows, the home that is a principal influence on the development of the main character, Vance Weston:

> The house, which was painted a dark brown, stood at the end of a short grass-grown drive, its front so veiled in the showering gold-green foliage of two ancient weeping willows that Vance could only catch, here and there, a hint of a steep rook, a jutting balcony, an aspiring turret. The facade, thus seen in trembling glimpses, as if it were as fluid as the trees, suggested vastness, fantasy, and secrecy. Green slopes of unmown grass, and heavy shrubberies of unpruned syringa and lilac, surrounded it; and beyond the view was closed in on all sides by trees and more trees.

The end of her sequel to *Hudson River Bracketed, The Gods Arrive,* finds Vance Weston returning to the Willows, and through the memories the old home evokes, he makes peace with his past.

The Vanderbilt Mansion in Hyde Park was also known to Edith and formed part of her youthful impressions. Although she mentions it some-

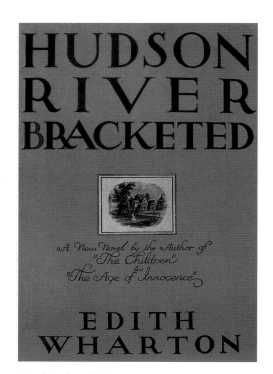

Book jacket, Hudson River Bracketed, *first edition, 1929*

what satirically in *The House of Mirth*, she was familiar with its architecture and interior decoration. The Vanderbilts were wealthier than Edith's family, but her family had a longer lineage in turn-of-the-century America and she probably considered the Vanderbilts somewhat nouveau riche, although she had a friendship with the George Vanderbilts, whose apartment she later rented in Paris. When writing of the Van Osburgh marriage, Van Osburgh probably being a code name for Vanderbilt, in *The House of Mirth*, Wharton humorously notes: "The Van Osburgh marriage was celebrated in the village church near the paternal estate on the Hudson. It was the 'simple country wedding' to which guests are convoyed in special trains, and from which the hordes of the uninvited have to be fended off by the intervention of the police." Despite this quote and other veiled references to the ostentation of the Vanderbilts, Wharton probably found quite a bit to admire in the architecture, interiors, and Italian-style gardens of the Vanderbilts' Hudson Valley villa.

Frederick William Vanderbilt, the grandson of Cornelius Vanderbilt, made this estate his country home from 1895 to 1938. Designed by Charles Follen McKim, the mansion was constructed in the Italian Renaissance style, which is also reflected in its interior design and furnishings. The four-story, fifty-room mansion is built of concrete and steel, faced with cut stone. Stanford White was instrumental in decorating the principal rooms of the first floor with antiques he had purchased during an 1897 trip to London, Paris, Florence, and Rome. These furnishings probably include the carved-wood dining-room ceiling, a large Ispahan rug and stone chimney breasts for the dining room, Renaissance chairs in the entrance hall, and marble columns in the drawing room. White was working in the style Wharton and Codman praised in *The Decoration of Houses*, published the very year that White was furnishing part of the Vanderbilt Mansion. Some of the other rooms of the mansion are also artfully designed but perhaps not always in the style favored by Wharton and Codman. Georges Glaezner decorated Frederick Vanderbilt's bedroom in a rather eclectic style using furniture of Spanish influence and a contemporary 1890s desk. The gold drawing room was also designed by Glaezner as an eighteenth-century French salon with Louis XV furnishings. Ogden Codman decorated Louise Vanderbilt's bedroom in French eighteenth-century reproduction furniture from the workshops of the late-nineteenth-century Parisian cabinetmaker Paul Sormani, who contributed the commodes and writing desk. The other furnishings are also reproductions of French eighteenth-century pieces. This was certainly a room that would have pleased Wharton. Several of the guest bedrooms, such as the blue room and the mauve room, are also thought to reflect the design

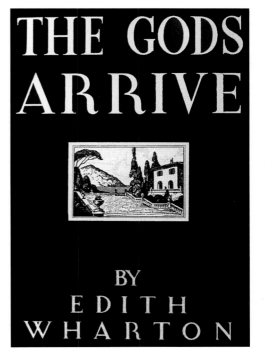

Book jacket, The Gods Arrive, *first edition, 1932*

Vanderbilt Mansion:
grand staircase, gold
drawing room, Louise
Vanderbilt's bedroom

principles of Codman. Common to both the blue and mauve rooms, for example, is a distinct color scheme and use of French-style furnishings, generally from the eighteenth century.

The grounds and gardens of the mansion are also worthy of note. There are over twenty types of trees on the grounds, which feature a pavilion designed by McKim, Mead & White in the fall of 1895. The pavilion's design is based on classical Greek architecture with functional adaptations. The Vanderbilts used the pavilion while the mansion was being completed and later to house an overflow of guests. The gardener's cottage and tool house predate the Vanderbilt era and were designed by the Boston architects John H. Sturgis and Charles Brigham in 1875. The Italian gardens include the rose garden, the cherry walk and pool gardens, and the greenhouse gardens. Also on the grounds are the McKim, Mead & White–designed main entrance gate, gatehouse, river gate, and river gatehouse.

Wharton was also familiar with the Mills Mansion near the Hudson in Staatsburg. The rooms of the mansion suggest the hall, drawing room, dining room, and terrace of the fictional mansion Bellomont, which appears in numerous scenes of *The House of Mirth*. The heroine, Lily Bart, often remarks on these rooms and their relationship to her emotional state. After an evening of bridge, at which she lost more than she could afford, Lily delays before going to bed: "Feeling no desire for the self-communion which awaited her in her room, she lingered on the broad stairway, looking down into the hall below . . . The hall was arcaded, with a gallery supported on columns of pale yellow marble. Tall clumps of flowering plants were grouped against a background of dark foliage in the angles of the walls." In a happier mood the grounds of Bellomont are described: "Everything in her surroundings ministered to feelings of ease and amenity. The windows stood open to the sparkling freshness of the September morning, and between the yellow boughs she caught a perspective of hedges and parterres leading by degrees of lessening formality to the free undulations of the park."

Lily also makes a keen observation of the library at Bellomont and of its owners, which have a surprising similarity to the library and owners of the Mills Mansion. In *Stanford White's New York*, Lowe writes: "The Mills' mansion's splendid spaces included a library, short on books but long on pilasters and paneling." Edith Wharton, through Lily Bart, describes the library at Bellomont:

> The library was almost the only surviving portion of the old manor-house of Bellomont: a long spacious room, revealing the traditions of the mother-country in its classically cased doors, the Dutch tiles of the chimney, and elaborate hob-grate with its shining brass urns. A few family portraits . . . hung between the

shelves lined with pleasantly shabby books; books mostly contemporaneous with the ancestors in question to which the subsequent Trenors had made no perceptible additions. The library for Bellomont was in fact never used for reading, though it had a certain popularity as a smoking-room or a quiet retreat for flirtation.

The Mills Mansion, like Bellomont, has as its core an older home of the Livingston family that had been inherited by Ruth Livingston Mills. This home was in the Greek Revival style. McKim, Mead & White enlarged and remodeled this base into a Beaux-Arts palace of sixty-five rooms and fourteen bathrooms. The renovations were completed in 1897. The mansion is constructed of brick with a stucco facade adorned with an impressive portico, pilasters, balustrades, fluted columns, and floral swags. The sumptuously decorated interior is primarily in the styles of seventeenth- and eighteenth-century France. Numerous Louis XV and Louis XVI pieces are featured. Decorative elements such as parquet floors, molded-plaster ceilings, marble fireplaces, and oak paneling dominate many rooms. In the center of the mansion is a six-columned portico, a testament to its classical treatment. Also in keeping with the classical architecture of the mansion, there were many objects of art on display from ancient Greece, Europe, and the Far East.

The natural landscape and grounds of the Mills Mansion contribute to its grandeur. The house is sited on a low hillside with a view of the Hudson's east shore and of both the Catskill and Shawangunk Mountains. Ruth and Ogden Mills spent only the autumn months at this home, but autumn is one of the most inspiring seasons in the Hudson Valley. It is autumn when Lily Bart in *The House of Mirth* enjoys the view from Bellomont's terrace:

Mills Mansion, Staatsburg, New York, circa 1900

> Seating herself on the upper step of the terrace, Lily leaned her head against the honeysuckle wreathing the balustrade. The fragrance of the late blossoms seemed an emanation of the tranquil scene, a landscape tutored to the last degree of rural elegance. In the foreground glowed the warm tints of the gardens. Beyond the lawn, with its pyramidal pale-gold maples and velvety firs, sloped pastures dotted with cattle; and through a long glade the river widened like a lake under the silver light of September.

*Mills Mansion: back
and front facades*

Wharton's first glimpses of post–Civil War Newport came in her early childhood, and she was certainly a full participant in Newport society after her debut in 1879. The young set spent their days at Newport riding, playing lawn tennis and croquet, and swimming. Young men fished, sailed, and played polo and golf. Young women enjoyed archery contests, a spectacle that intrigued the young Edith Jones, who reports in her memoir: "Those archery meetings greatly heightened my infantile desire to 'tell a story,' and the young gods and goddesses strolling across the Edgerston lawn were the prototypes of my first novels." The summer inhabitants of Newport enjoyed gala balls and attending yacht races. Activity often centered around the Newport Casino, commissioned by the publisher of the *New York Herald,* James Gordon Bennett, and designed by McKim, Mead & White. McKim designed the shingle-clad facade on Bellevue Avenue, Newport's major thoroughfare, and White designed the grounds, including the lawn-tennis courts, veranda, stage for entertainments, and dark-green treillage. The facade of the casino features an asymmetrical arrangement of dormers, a pitched roof, and a tower equipped with a Tiffany clock for the convenience of the lawn-tennis players. The casino is somewhat eclectic in its architectural elements and features a mix of Queen Anne, American Colonial, and British Raj styles with a touch of Japanese influence.

*Newport Casino
ca. 1900*

Wharton certainly frequented the Newport Casino, but it may not have influenced her architectural preferences as much as the other Newport homes with which she was familiar. Her parents' own home, Pencraig, was a substantial summer "cottage." When Edith and her family returned from Europe in 1872 to the Old New York she thought rather ugly, she found her family's summers at Pencraig refreshing. Pencraig had lawns, meadows, flowers, and even a pony to ride and terriers to romp with, and as Wharton notes in *A Backward Glance,* "a sheltered cove to bathe in, flower-beds spicy with 'carnation, lily, rose,' and a kitchen-garden crimson with strawberries and sweet as honey with Seckel pears." Pencraig appealed to the young Edith's appreciation of natural beauty:

The roomy and pleasant house of Pencraig was surrounded by a verandah wreathed in clematis and honeysuckle, and below it a lawn sloped to a deep daisied meadow, beyond which were a private bathing-beach and boat-landing. From the landing we used to fish for "scuppers" and porgies, succulent little fish that were grilled or fired for high tea; and off the rocky point lay my father's and brother's "cat-boats," the graceful wide sailed craft that flecked the bay like sea-gulls.

Edith used other cottage-mansions in her fiction. Louis Auchincloss speculates in *Edith Wharton: A Woman in Her Time* that in her Pulitzer Prize–winning novel of 1870s society, *The Age of Innocence*, the character Julius Beaufort's Newport summer home is a composite of Oaklawn, the home of Charles H. Russel, and Belcourt, the home of August Belmont. In the novel, an archery contest takes place on the lawn of this Newport cottage, which she describes clearly:

> The small bright lawn stretched away smoothly to the big bright sea. The turf was hemmed with an edge of scarlet geranium and coleus, and cast-iron vases painted in chocolate color, standing at intervals along the winding path that led to the sea, looped their garlands of petunia and ivy geranium above the neatly raked gravel. Halfway between the edge of the cliff and the square wooden house (which was also chocolate-colored, but with the tin roof of the verandah striped in yellow and brown to represent an awning) two large targets had been placed against a background of shrubbery.

Wharton was also familiar with the more elegant mansions of Newport, as some of the elements of their gala rooms figure prominently in *The Decoration of Houses*. Several Newport mansions were designed in the classical style by architects Wharton and Codman admired. Among these stately homes are the Breakers, Marble House, and Rosecliff.

Period photographs of the exterior and interior of Pencraig, the Jones family home in Newport

Cornelius Vanderbilt, son of William Henry Vanderbilt and grandson of the commodore, commissioned Richard Morris Hunt to design a summer villa for his family. The original Breakers, purchased in 1885, was destroyed by fire in 1892. Edith was at the Breakers when the fire broke out. Clarice Stasz reports in *The Vanderbilt Women: Dynasty of Wealth, Glamour, and Tragedy:* "On November 25, a cold, windy afternoon, Alice welcomed Pussy Jones, now wed to Edward

*Mills Mansion: library,
dining room*

East facade of the
Breakers, Newport,
Rhode Island

Wharton. While they gathered, quietly talking, an unexpected racket arose from the servants' quarters. The house was on fire, the voices shouted; they must flee immediately."

The plan for the new villa was based on the Renaissance architecture of Turin and Genoa. Work on this seventy-room, four-story limestone structure was completed in 1895. It is noted for its symmetry as well as its scale. The main hall is forty-five feet high and the east wall, almost entirely of glass, presents a view through the double loggia stretching to the sea. The two-story dining salon has arched ceilings adorned with cherubs and gilded bronze. The main glass chandelier is suspended from the ceiling and other chandeliers are attached to alabaster columns. The hardwood floor is par-

tially covered by a rug of Oriental design. The family dining room features a similar floor treatment and wall sconces against pale green walls with gold decorative details and a marble-mirrored fireplace. The library has a grand fireplace and a stone chimney piece from a French château. The music and billiard rooms are also decorated in a lavish but harmonious fashion. Several of the bedrooms in the Breakers were decorated by Ogden Codman, who was introduced to Alice Vanderbilt by Wharton.

Richard Morris Hunt also designed Marble House as the summer residence of William K. and Alva Vanderbilt. Constructed of white marble, modeled after the Petit Trianon at Versailles, and similar in architectural style to both the Temple of Apollo at Heliopolis, Greece, and the White House, the mansion was completed in 1892. Both the interior and the exterior boast an abundance of marble, including

The great hall at the Breakers

golden Siena and pink Numidian marble, among other types. Period furnishings, chiefly Louis XIV and Louis XV styles, sculpture, and other objects of art were provided by the Paris shop of J. Allard and Son. Wharton and Codman appreciated the attributes of Marble House, and regarded it as a significant work by an American architect in the classical style.

The Stanford White–designed small-scale version of Louis XIV's Grand Trianon at Versailles, called Rosecliff, was constructed for Theresa and Hermann Oelrichs. The mansion was not completed until 1902, after the 1897 publication of *The Decoration of Houses*. Wharton was probably familiar with it from the time she and Teddy spent at their own Newport home, Land's End. Rosecliff is constructed of brick faced with white terra-

The great hall at Marble House, Newport, Rhode Island (opposite); the ballroom and salon, or reception room, at Rosecliff, Newport

*Marble House
(opposite);
Rosecliff*

cotta tiles, and its facade features double Ionic columns and French windows. The focal point of the vestibule is a heart-shaped staircase, a striking prelude to the largest ballroom in Newport, with a ceiling of painted clouds. An air of spaciousness also presides over the dining room and the salon, both of which have elegant central fireplaces. The ballroom and the salon have architectural elements and furnishings generally in accordance with the principles espoused in *The Decoration of Houses*. The current grounds at Rosecliff are notable not only for the restored rose garden but also for their numerous elegant statues, fountains, and garden ornaments. Augustus Saint-Gaudens designed a *court d'amour* for the grounds based on a landscape design for the gardens at Versailles.

First impressions are often lasting ones, and the impressions of Old New York, the scenic Hudson Valley, and fashionable Newport were certainly formative ones for the young Edith and influenced her understanding of her society and its subsequent portrayal in her literary work. Interestingly, Wharton's later works are often set in the times of her childhood. Her first impressions certainly influenced her writings on architecture, interiors, and gardens and also the architectural and decorative plans for her own homes.

First Homes
1885–1900

IN THE EARLY YEARS OF EDITH AND TEDDY'S MARRIAGE, THEY WERE OCCUPIED IN finding suitable residences that would complement their status as a young married couple. They needed elegant spaces in which they could entertain their friends and relatives and house the furniture and decorative objects they acquired on their European trips. It was customary for couples of their social standing to have both a house in town and a residence in Newport, Long Island, or the Berkshires. The Whartons' first country home was a cottage belonging to Edith's parents in fashionable Newport.

PENCRAIG COTTAGE

View ca. 1885

PENCRAIG COTTAGE

After Edith and Teddy were married in 1885 they spent part of each year at Pencraig Cottage, which was on the grounds of Pencraig, her family's summer home. In her memoir Wharton writes: "My first care was to create a home of my own; and a few months after our marriage my husband and I moved into a little cottage in the grounds of Pencraig, and rearranged it in accordance with our tastes . . . So we settled down at Pencraig Cottage, and for a few years always lived there from June till February; and I was too busy with my little house and garden ever to find the time long." In *The Mount: A Historic Structure Report*, Scott Marshall discusses Edith's first homes and describes Pencraig Cottage as "a modest two-and-a-half-story wooden frame house in the Italianate style. The center section was three bays wide; on either side were irregularly shaped wings. The most dominant exterior feature was an airy verandah in the more ornate Victorian style, clearly a later addition to the building." Marshall also describes what is known of the furnishings in the first home that Wharton decorated herself.

Despite the Victorian floral wallpaper—typical of the period—which Edith would soon abhor in *The Decoration of Houses*, the rooms convey a style of living, which emphasized comfort and practicality. The furniture was not heavy or overstuffed nor were the floors overwhelmed with thick carpets or the walls with excess decoration or pictures. Personal touches included bookcases filled with books (books for reading—not for mere decoration), carefully selected objets d'art and a table heaped with books and magazines. In addition there were numerous floral arrangements about the room, no doubt picked, arranged and placed by the mistress herself. Photographs of family and friends abounded on the mantel, bookcase and on tables.

Life in cozy Pencraig Cottage was interrupted by exciting plans for European travel. As Wharton notes in *A Backward Glance:* "Every year we went abroad in February for four months of travel; and it was then that I really felt alive." In happy anticipation of her extensive fall European wanderings, Edith would read various volumes and in this period she discovered James Fergusson's *History of Architecture,* noting in her memoir: "It shed on my misty haunting sense of the beauty of old buildings the light of historical and technical precision, and cleared and extended my horizon." Edith also discovered Italian eighteenth-century furniture at about the same time. Shortly after her marriage she sat for a portrait by Teddy's old friend Julian Story in his Paris studio and noticed an elegant armchair. Story informed her that the chair was eighteenth-century Venetian. Edith's imagination was stirred, as the eighteenth-century arts were generally felt to belong to France and the *cinquecento* was considered the Italian period. The elegant piece of Venetian furniture led Edith to explore the arts of the eighteenth century in Italy. As she writes in her memoir: "The new turn thus given to my curiosity made us devote our subsequent holidays to the study of eighteenth-century painting and architecture in Italy. In these pleasant explorations Egerton Winthrop was our constant companion." Winthrop, a generation older than Edith, was of the same lineage as her family, his ancestry rooted in Revolutionary America. They shared a love of books, architecture, and art, which set them apart from fashionable Old New York and Newport society. After Wharton discovered the Italian *settecento*, Winthrop encouraged her in its study, and when they were part of the same traveling party in Italy, he helped her to purchase Venetian furniture that was to be displayed in her Newport home Land's End. Winthrop was representative of the Old New York of Edith's parents, so much so that Richard Guy Wilson's essay "Edith and Ogden: Writing, Decoration, and Architecture" in *Ogden Codman and the Decoration of Houses* suggests that he was the model for the society gossip Sillerton Jackson in *The Age of Innocence* and in the novellas of the *Old New York* series. Wilson also describes Winthrop's New York home on East Thirty-third Street, known and admired by Wharton, as a Richard Morris Hunt home in the French Second Empire style with every article of furniture imported from France.

In this manner Wharton's tastes in French and Italian architecture and furniture continued developing. Her intellectual interest in Italy continued as well and, along with her travels during her early married years, was the foundation of Italian themes that would later surface in *The Decoration of Houses*, *Italian Villas and Their Gardens*, *Italian Backgrounds*, and her first novel, *The Valley of Decision*, which is set in northern Italy.

An Aegean cruise was the most exciting travel adventure the Whartons experienced during their early married years. They joined a friend, James Van Alen, also from a distinguished Old New York family, on a chartered yacht, even though the four-month cruise would exhaust their joint income for the entire year. The Whartons proceeded undaunted and had a rewarding trip throughout the Aegean islands, where they were probably among the first American visitors to some remote spots. Wharton had the opportunity to view Greek classical architecture, which added to her overall understanding of the subject. She also enjoyed yachting, a subject she infused into her fiction, particularly in the Dorset yacht trip in *The House of Mirth* and in the protagonist Kate Clephane's invitation to a yachting excursion in *The Mother's Recompense.*

Fortunately for the Whartons, their financial situation was improved by an unexpected inheritance that Edith received from Joshua Jones, a cousin of her grandfather, Edward Renshaw Jones. Joshua Jones had led a sparse, eccentric, and reclusive existence for twenty years at the New York Hotel. At his death in March 1888, Edith and both of her brothers each inherited $120,000, a sum that at the time was sufficient to make Edith and Teddy financially secure. Edith, anxious to have a New York base of her own, rented a small house on Madison Avenue. Entrenched in her own surroundings in New York, she could seek out suitable companionship, and in this period she cultivated the friendship of Egerton Winthrop as well as Robert Minturn, a member in good standing of Old New York and a linguist and connoisseur of the arts; Ogden Codman Jr.; and Bayard Cutting, a railroad tycoon and collector of European art for both his New York and Long Island homes.

Wharton took up her own literary pursuits at this time, and shortly after she and Teddy moved into their rented New York house, three of her poems were accepted for publication in *Scribner's*. One of them, "The Last Giustiani," is set in eighteenth-century Venice, reflecting her interest in the Italy of that time. In May 1890 her short story "Mrs. Manstey's View" was also accepted for publication in *Scribner's*. In this story, a sense of place is predominant: Mrs. Manstey, a widow, resides in the back room of a New York boardinghouse and hopes to preserve her view of the gardens outside her window by protesting the construction of a building next door. The theme of the protection of beauty finds an echo in Lily Bart's boardinghouse window at the tragic close of *The House of Mirth*, when Lawrence Selden looks up at the boardinghouse and recognizes Lily's window—the only one with a flowerbox on the sill.

In 1891, after the Whartons returned from their summer travels to Paris, the French Riviera, Florence, and Venice, Edith submitted another story to *Scribner's*, entitled "The Fullness of Life." This title reflects the yearnings of the main character, who has not known such fulfillment. It can be read as Wharton's voicing of sadness and resignation at the lack of intellectual and physical satisfaction in her marriage. It contains a striking early example of the uses Wharton made of architecture and a sense of place in the psychological development of her characters. In this tale she writes:

> I have sometimes thought that a woman's nature is like a great house full of rooms: there is the hall, through which everyone passes in going in and out; the

882–884 PARK AVENUE

View in the 1890s

drawing room, where one receives formal visits; the sitting room, where members of the family come and go as they list; but beyond that, far beyond, are other rooms, the handles of whose doors are never turned; no one knows the way to them, no one knows whither they lead, and in the innermost room, the holy of holies, the soul sits alone and waits for a footstep that never comes.

This is the first indication in the fiction of the twenty-nine-year-old Edith that she finds married life lacking.

Teddy was not as intellectually complex as Edith, and by her own admission she had no knowledge of the physical aspects of marriage, as no one ever enlightened her on the subject. Teddy was interested in sports, social activities, and travel. He supported Edith's desire to take the Aegean cruise, even though it might have placed them in some financial difficulties. He encouraged her first writing attempts and publications. He expressed pride in her intellectual achievements, even though he probably did not completely see their scope. He found it amazing that someone who was so socially competent could be so intellectually inclined. He saw to various travel plans and to the upkeep of the various motorcars that they acquired. Teddy was probably a bit baffled by Edith's serious side and literary pursuits but during their early years together was congenial, and Edith had a certain maternal fondness for him. Unfortunately their limited compatibility did not outweigh their differences, as they were decidedly mismatched from the outset and the rigid behaviors of their social "tribe" did not ameliorate matters. Edith's growing independence, both financially and psychologically, cast a decidedly negative light on Teddy. Both Edith and Teddy, to their credit, tried to make the best of a bad business and in 1891 acquired their first home in New York City.

882–884 PARK AVENUE

In November 1891 Edith purchased a small townhouse at Fourth Avenue near the corner of Seventy-eighth Street. The house was so narrow, only between fifteen and sixteen feet wide, that Edith and Teddy at first rented it. Several years later they were able to purchase the house next door. The two were sufficient to house the Whartons and their staff. At that time Edith and Teddy moved into 884 Park Avenue, as the location was now called, and their staff took up residence in 882 Park. Edith was finally able to fashion her new home to her liking and took considerable pride in its furnishing. For almost a decade, this small home was the Wharton's winter residence. They spent the summers first at Land's End in Newport, which they acquired in March 1893, and later at The Mount in Lenox, Massachusetts. To facilitate their travels about town, the Whartons also purchased a carriage house at 111 East Seventy-seventh Street.

As Edith was beginning to spend more and more time writing, she was grateful for a home of her own in town in which she could devote herself to literary pursuits. She recalls in *A Backward Glance:* "I had grown very weary of our annual wanderings, and now that I had definite work to do I felt the need of a winter home where I could continue my writing, instead of having to pack up every autumn, as we had been doing for over fifteen years." She also mentions the satisfaction of decorating their tiny home:

> I had the amusement of adorning our sixteen-foot-wide house in New York with the modest spoils of our Italian travels, and my summers being quiet I did not so much mind the social demands of the winter. Besides, life in New York, with its theatres and opera, and its new interests of all kinds, was very different from the frivolity of Newport; and I was happy in my work, and in the sense of confidence in my powers.

Wharton's passion for writing and decorating continued. After they purchased their own home in Newport, Land's End, the Whartons consulted with Ogden Codman about alterations to it. At this time, Codman also became involved in plans for alterations to 882–884 Park Avenue. He provided elegant sketches for alterations to the facades of the townhouses and apparently made suggestions on combining the two. Unfortunately his plans were never carried out, but he did advise Edith on architectural elements, wallpaper, and furnishings and decorated the dining room. The parlor, or small drawing room, had a fireplace with mirrored mantel. The mirror was framed with a decorative border that was surmounted by an urn entwined with leaves. The walls were done in striped wallpaper, not in keeping with Wharton's later principles, as she was not fond of the use of paper wall coverings. The wall's striped design was repeated on the fabric of two armchairs. Scattered elegant tables, lamps, vases, statues, and decorative andirons completed the decorative elements along with a side mirror and paintings in round frames. Books were on a low shelf to the right of the fireplace and filled bookshelves are reflected in the mantel mirror. The dining room featured an elegant French marble fireplace with an ornamented mirror over the mantel. Furnishings included painted-wood dining chairs with cane seats, two dark wood cabinets, one on each side of the fireplace, elegant candlesticks, and a decorative clock. The prominent wallpaper appears to have been influenced by a taste for chinoiserie and had a colorful floral spring garden motif. At roughly the same time that Edith and Codman were decorating the Park Avenue residence, the Whartons were collaborating with Codman on the alterations to the exterior and the furnishings of their new Newport home, Land's End.

882–884 Park Avenue

Rendering of alterations to the facade (by Ogden Codman Jr.)

882–884 PARK AVENUE

Drawing room, dining room, and dining room fireplace ca. 1895

LAND'S END

With the help of the inheritance from her cousin, Edith and Teddy purchased property on Aquidneck Island; Wharton describes their home there, Land's End on Ledge Road in Newport, in *A Backward Glance:*

> Thanks to my cousin's testamentary discernment my husband and I had been able to buy a home of our own at Newport. It was an ugly wooden house with half an acre of rock and illimitable miles of Atlantic Ocean; for as its name, "Land's End," denoted, it stood on the edge of Rhode Island's easternmost cliffs, and our windows looked straight across to the west coast of Ireland. I disliked the relaxing and depressing climate, and the vapid watering-place amusements in which the days were wasted; but I loved Land's End, with its windows framing the endlessly changing moods of the misty Atlantic, and the night-long sound of the surges against the cliffs.

The property of Land's End also contained a stable, a small frame building apart from the main home, and relatively extensive grounds. Little could be changed of the architecture of the main house, but the grounds and interior could certainly be improved. To this end Edith and Teddy consulted frequently with Ogden Codman. As Wharton recalls in her memoir:

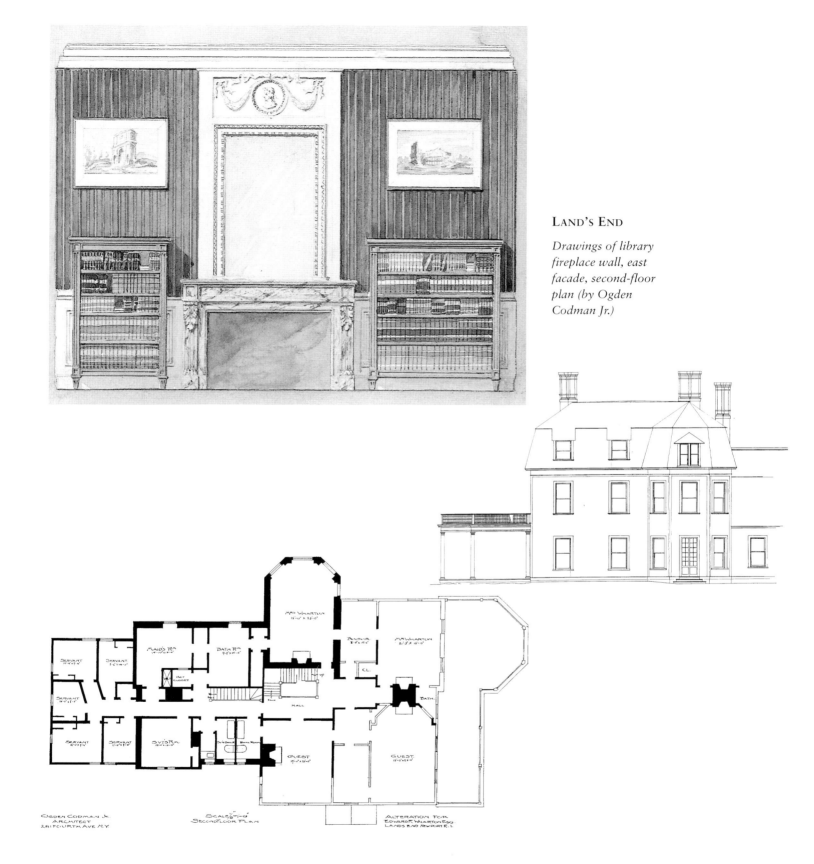

LAND'S END

Drawings of library fireplace wall, east facade, second-floor plan (by Ogden Codman Jr.)

LAND'S END

Drawing of terrace trellis (by Ogden Codman Jr.)

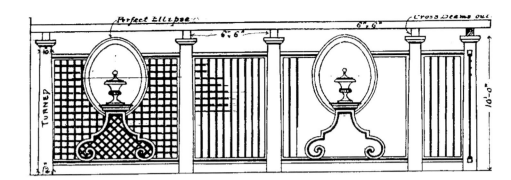

The outside of the house was incurably ugly, but we helped it to a certain dignity by laying out a circular court with high hedges and trellis-work niches (the whole promptly done way with by our successors!); and within doors there were interesting possibilities. My husband and I talked them over with a clever young Boston architect, Ogden Codman, and we asked him to alter and decorate the house—a somewhat new departure, since the architects of that day looked down on house-decoration as a branch of dress-making, and left the field to the upholsterers, who crammed every room with curtains, lambrequins, jardinieres of artificial plants, wobbly velvet-covered tables littered with silver gew-gaws, and festoons of lace on mantlepieces and dressing-tables.

The Whartons and Codman worked to overcome these pitfalls. Codman prepared architectural plans for alterations to the east facade, a revised second-story floor plan, drawings of architectural elements for the library, and designs of niches and trellises for the grounds. His influence can be seen in the furnishings of the library, dining room, drawing room, glass room, and Edith's boudoir as well as in the landscape design. Edith's niece Beatrix Jones Farrand, a landscape architect, was probably also involved in the design of the court and garden.

The work on the remodeling and furnishing of Land's End took several years. Land's End does not completely follow the principles that Wharton and Codman were to espouse in *The Decoration of Houses,* but they had to work within certain architectural constraints. As Richard Guy Wilson aptly notes in "Edith and Ogden: Writing, Decoration, and Architecture," "Constrained by the existing shell, some rooms, such as the drawing room, appear too low for their breadth; the proportions are mean," and "In both [dining and sitting rooms] the plaster ceiling lacked any relation to the room below and asserted too much weight."

Other elements of the interior furnishings and planning of the grounds were more successful. The hall and staircase were simple, elegant, and understated. The library had a mantel mirror, medallion, and scrollwork designed by Codman, but the furniture, while comfortable, was not in keeping with the eighteenth-century furniture found in the other rooms. The research of

LAND'S END

Hallway (ca. 1900),
library (ca. 1893),
dining room (ca. 1900)

Scott Marshall shows that many of the furnishings of the Land's End library were transferred to The Mount. The comfortable furniture was used in the library at The Mount and the classically inspired medallion designed by Codman was re-created in Teddy Wharton's den there. The library panels were painted pink and the bookshelves, although in darkwood—pale wood is recommended in *The Decoration of Houses*—were in proportion to the other elements of the room. Small-scale paintings adorn the paneled walls in the library. Marshall's research also indicates that the eagle andirons in the fireplace at Land's End were probably those Edith referred to in *A Backward Glance* as belonging to her great-grandfather General Ebenezer Stevens.

Wilson in "Edith and Ogden" also reports that: "Simple eighteenth-century French and Italian furniture occupied the dining and sitting rooms, but the wall coverings of damask—which Wharton and Codman would soon denounce as unsanitary—had a heavy and bold pattern resembling flock." Other than this flaw and the disproportion of the ceiling, the sitting, or drawing, room was harmoniously decorated and comfortable. Even with these drawbacks, the dining room had a certain elegance and light quality. The white-painted wood furniture, tasteful fireplace, ceiling moldings, and wall sconces added to its appeal. As was soon to be advised in *The Decoration of Houses*, the rug had a pleasing pattern and could easily be removed for cleaning. Scott Marshall's *The Mount* shows that the furniture of the Land's End dining room was transferred to The Mount and its carpet was used in The Mount's library.

Edith's boudoir at Land's End had toile curtains and toile-upholstered eighteenth-century armchairs. Its sense of classical proportion was underscored by an elegant fireplace, with a mirror over the mantel encased in delicate scrollwork, matching wall sconces,

LAND'S END

Drawing room and glass room ca. 1900

wall tables, and vases. Perhaps the glass-walled verandah of Land's End was its most successful room. Codman decided to enclose a porch, making it into a second sitting room, to take advantage of its ocean view through its elegant spare furnishings and understated floor treatment. A beautifully carved Louis XV wood writing table and a statue of a cherub were the interior focal points, but they do not detract from the ocean view, as they are well placed in the sparsely furnished and tranquil setting.

The remodeled grounds also added to the appeal of Land's End. Codman designed decorative garden niches and trellises that distracted the eye from the views of the house that he and the Whartons found unsatisfactory. Both Codman and Wharton were influenced in their plans for the garden by their travels to Italy. As Richard Guy Wilson notes in "Edith and Ogden": "Though the exterior of the house remained awkward, a circular forecourt and hedge added formality to the main approach and masked the service wing. On the garden side terraces and paths were graded. Wooden trellises, pergolas, and lath niches . . . masked the rambling house from the formal garden."

While renovations were underway at Land's End, Wharton and Codman made the decision to collaborate on *The Decoration of Houses*. They found that they had similar ideas on simplicity and harmony in architecture and disliked the overcrowded, cluttered look of late-Victorian interior decoration. As Wharton reports in her memoir:

> Codman shared my dislike of these sumptuary excesses, and thought as I did that interior decoration should be simple and architectural; and finding that we had the same views we drifted, I hardly know how, toward the notion of putting them into a book. We went into every detail of our argument; the idea, novel at the time though now self-evident that the interior of a house is as much a part of the organic structure as the outside, and that its treatment ought, in the same measure, to be based on right proportion, balance of door and window spacing, and simple unconfused lines. We developed this argument logically, and I think forcibly, and then sat down to write the book.

LAND'S END

Gardens ca. 1900

Their book was written during 1896 and 1897 and was placed with Edith's literary publisher, Scribner's. Walter Berry, a distant relative of Edith's, helped in editing the book. (Walter and Edith were probably in love with each other in their youth, but they did not decide to marry; they remained fast friends throughout their lives. Berry often read Edith's manuscripts and encouraged and critiqued her literary work.) The architect Charles McKim also read *Decoration* before its publication and was enthusiastic about it. *Decoration* was well received on its publication and was reprinted in England and New York.

In addition to her decorating and literary pursuits at this time, Edith also opened her first home suitable to entertaining on a larger scale; many of her guests would play a significant role in her literary and personal development. In *Edith Wharton: A Biography*, R. W. B. Lewis summarizes Edith's emergence as a hostess in her first full-sized home:

> Among the first guests to be entertained at Land's End were Paul Bourget, the French novelist and essayist, and his wife, the former Minnie David. Their visit in the early autumn of 1893 was a momentous one for Edith Wharton. She had been perfecting her role of hostess and had at dinner a procession of Astors and Van Alens, Belmonts and Goelets; but she was growing more depressed than ever by her Newport neighbors. They seemed to her, in her own phrase, hermetically sealed off from those cultural movements which in Europe, as she understood, touched and affected even the socially frivolous. With the Bourgets, literature and thought entered her living room almost for the first time, and on an imposing scale.

Article on Paul Bourget, New York Herald *(Paris edition), 1897*

Bourget was traveling in the United States to research articles for the *New York Herald*. While in Newport, he and his wife visited Land's End several times. He and Edith discussed Italian furnishings and literary topics as well as the techniques of writing. Bourget and Wharton established a relationship that was to flourish again in the Faubourg St. Germain, where the Bourgets had an apartment on rue Vaneau that the Whartons visited shortly after they had met in Newport and subsequently when the Whartons stayed in or near the faubourg. At this time of her literary development, Edith's friendship with Bourget was not only intellectually satisfying, but his contacts in Europe helped to further her travel reporting and writing. Bourget introduced her to Mrs. Violet Page (Vernon Lee), author of *Studies of the Eighteenth Century in Italy, Belcaro,* and *Euphorion,* which Wharton called "three of my best-loved companions of the road." Vernon Lee lived in Florence and offered Edith assistance in locating and gaining access to various homes that were to be featured in *Italian Villas and Their Gardens.* As Wharton recalls in *A Backward Glance:* "Vernon Lee's long familiarity with the Italian country-side, and the wide circle of her Italian friendships, made it easy for her to guide me to the right places, and put me in relation with people who could enable me to visit them. She herself took me to nearly all the villas I wished to visit near Florence, and it was thanks to her recommendation that wherever I went, from the Lakes to the Roman Campagna, I found open doors and a helpful hospitality."

The fiction Wharton completed before the construction of The Mount included the novella *The Touchstone* (1900) and two volumes of short stories, *The Greater Inclination* (1899) and *Crucial Instances* (1901). In *The Touchstone* the main character, Stephen Glennard, buys his happiness by publishing the letters of an accomplished woman novelist, which were written to him before she died. In the short story "A Journey," a woman faces a new phase of her life when her husband dies on a train trip. In "The Pelican" a mother who has given lectures on cultural themes to support her son is confronted by him as an adult and asked why she continues to give lectures when he hasn't needed support for many years. His mother feels that she must continue to do so for her grandchildren, as she is reluctant to give up her maternal role. "The Duchess at Prayer" is set at an Italian villa, which along with its gardens, is extensively described. The other stories of *Crucial Instances* are set in locales indicative of Edith's travels and interests, including New England, London, and an Old New York drawing room. In "The Moving Finger" Grancy's beloved wife's portrait has been painted by Claydon. When she dies Grancy forces Claydon to update her painting so that she, in her portrait, might grow old with him. Mrs. Grancy's portrait predicts Grancy's death, after which Claydon restores the portrait to its original evocation of Mrs. Grancy, a woman he had also loved, as past and present are commingled.

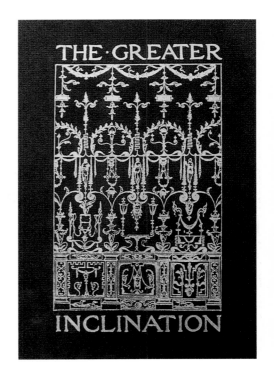

Book cover, The Greater Inclination, *first edition, 1899*

R. W. B. Lewis, in his biography of Wharton, notes that the major themes of the work she completed at this time focus on "the fairly remote past and involve an effort to achieve or restore continuity . . . between the past and the present." In a sense this theme may be viewed as an attempt by the author to understand her own identity and sense of physical and emotional place in American society. As Lewis aptly writes:

> Edith Wharton, whose handling of the elements of "place" in her fiction was one of her strongest features, tended in her life to dramatize a change of personal fortunes or of her sense of herself by entering into a new scene of residence. Her first experience of residence, a decade earlier, had led to the rental and then the purchase of a home in New York, and to another one at a remote point in Newport. Now, as she was becoming established as Edith Wharton, a gifted writer of fiction, she was taken by a desire to shift residence again. This time she would build a home of her own from the ground up. Lenox, with its bracing atmosphere and magnificent surroundings, was to be the place.

The Mount
1901–1911

Around the turn of the century, Edith Wharton grew tired of the trivial pursuits of Newport and longed for a more substantial country home whose grounds and villa could be of her own design and decoration—a place where she could have the serenity to continue her writing and accommodate, on a grander scale, the visits of her more recent literary acquaintances as well as long-time friends and relatives. Her successful early novels gave her the financial security to realize her hopes in the purchase of property in Lenox, Massachusetts, where her elegant new home would be constructed.

PROPERTY AND PLANS

In February 1901 Edith began negotiating for a property of 113 acres called Laurel Lake Farm in Lenox. It belonged to the Sargent family, and Wharton's dealings were with Georgiana Sargent, a watercolorist. By June, the negotiations were complete, and the construction of The Mount began soon thereafter. Coincidentally, Edith's mother Lucretia died in Paris and left Edith a trust fund that, with her other funds, would provide her with a comfortable yearly income.

Ogden Codman Jr. was the obvious choice for architect, but wrangling over his fees, which Edith deemed exorbitant, eventually excluded him from this commission, although he did work on the initial planning and interior decoration. Francis V. L. Hoppin of New York became the designer of The Mount. The plans were based on Belton House, the home of Lord Brownlow in Lincolnshire, England, a design attributed to Christopher Wren; Richard Guy Wilson, however, posits that William Winde was the architect and

William Stanton the contractor. Wharton most probably visited Belton House on her travels and found it particularly appealing.

Edith was thrilled to have the opportunity to put her principles of architecture, interior design, and landscape gardening to use in a home that she could oversee from plan to execution. She was also anxious to have a tranquil setting for her writing. She recalls in her memoir:

> We sold our Newport house, and built one near Lenox, in the hills of western Massachusetts, and at last I escaped from watering-place trivialities to the real country . . . for life in the country is the only state which has always completely satisfied me, and I had never been allowed to gratify it, even for a few weeks at a time. Now I was to know the joys of six or seven months a year among fields and woods of my own.

PHYSICAL SETTING

The 113 acres purchased from the Sargent family and fifteen acres Edith purchased later were situated at the southwest corner of Lenox and edged into the neighboring town of Lee. Wharton describes the site in *A Backward Glance:* "On a slope overlooking the dark waters and densely wooded shores of Laurel Lake we built a spacious and dignified house to which we gave the name of my great grandfather's place, The Mount." The estate is described in Scott Marshall's *The Mount: A Historic Structure Report:* "From the entrance gate on the north to the lake border at the southeastern termination, the estate included woodland, pasture, an orchard, manicured lawns, formal gardens and at least ten outbuildings in addition to the mansion." Many of these areas and structures are no longer present at The Mount, although some may be restored by Edith Wharton Restoration, which is currently engaged in this work. (The group also presents tours of the property and dramatizations of Edith Wharton's fiction there.)

The exterior and interior of The Mount are at present partially restored, and work is being planned to restore the gardens. Among the original structures of The Mount that are no longer present are the front gate and the pond building. The greenhouse is in disrepair and only ruins of the springhouse are visible. Two interesting original structures are the gatehouse, or caretaker's cottage, and the stables. The wood-frame and stucco gatehouse is painted white with green shutters and features a classical entrance porch. The stable's facade is white stucco. Scott Marshall describes it: "It is seven bays wide . . . The center bay . . . is topped by an ornamental Flemish gable. All windows are double-sashed. Second-story dormer windows pierce

THE MOUNT

View in 1906

the roof edge and are capped by gabled roofs while the center of the Flemish gable features a round window." Both the exterior colors and architectural elements of the gatehouse and stable echo and blend with The Mount itself. The original farm buildings, built prior to the Whartons' tenancy, have been altered over the years to serve a variety of other purposes. Finally, there is a modern cottage (1965) on the grounds.

Wharton summed up the physical and emotional appeal of The Mount in her memoir: "There was a big kitchen-garden with a grape pergola, a little farm, and a flower-garden outspread below the wide terrace overlooking the lake. There for over ten years I lived and gardened and wrote contentedly."

EXTERIORS

Construction on The Mount began in July 1901, and the Whartons were able to move in in September 1902. Ogden Codman was involved in the initial stages of The Mount's conception, and his influence, as well as that of Francis Hoppin, is apparent. Edith's niece Beatrix Farrand (then Jones) was involved with the garden planning. The mansion is set into a hillside. This feature and the H-shaped plan can be at least partially attributed to Codman. In addition, the H-shaped plan is consistent with the plan of the seventeenth-century Belton House. Both Codman and Hoppin (and most probably Wharton) were familiar with Belton House, as their previous commissions demonstrate.

The exteriors of The Mount show it to be a grand home with many influences. Modeled after an English country estate, it boasts a courtyard in the French tradition, an Italianate terrace, and the green-and-white exterior color scheme of a proper New England estate. It is constructed of white-painted stucco with green window shutters. The forecourt walls of white-painted brick provide a transition from the drive to the west facade of the mansion. Although the forecourt serves a crucial structural function—a retaining wall for The Mount's hillside site—it also has the aesthetic function of a French-style courtyard. The forecourt apparently contained statues, of which no photographic documentation survives. The forecourt encloses the formal part of the home and excludes the servants' entrance.

The forecourt leads to the west facade of The Mount, and from the forecourt the ground floor, main floor, bedroom floor, and attic stories are visible. The finished construction shows changes from Hoppin's architectural drawings. The five windows on the architect's rendering for the main-floor gallery were reduced to three. In the interests of symmetry there is a false ("blind") window on the main floor of the west facade to the left of the gallery windows; its shutters are always closed.

Visible on the north facade are the main and upper floors and part of the terrace, while the east facade is the most dramatic. The architect's original sketch shows five French doors in the drawing room, though only three were constructed. Two blind windows are included, however, and give the impression of five full French doors, at least from the exterior. The east facade also features an Italian-style terrace that runs the length of the north facade and wraps around a small length of the south facade as well. The most appealing views of The Mount's east facade are from the terrace path or garden areas; the terrace reflects The Mount's hillside setting, as it is placed into the slope at various elevations.

The terrace and the hillside meet at a point opposite the French windows of Teddy Wharton's den. The terrace is constructed of brick in a herringbone pattern with a marble base and hand railings. The balusters and piers are a combination of stucco and brick. The other decorative elements of the terrace (no longer present) consisted of a series of obelisks and two marble statues in the classical style. The terrace descends to the gardens and lawns by means of a Palladian staircase constructed of the same materials as the terrace, along with white-marble panels. The staircase ends at a niche containing a fountain where water flowed from a decorative lion's head.

The dining room, drawing room, library, and Teddy Wharton's den all open to the terrace. Due to its tranquil and varied views as well as its inherent aesthetic qualities, the terrace was used for dining, entertaining,

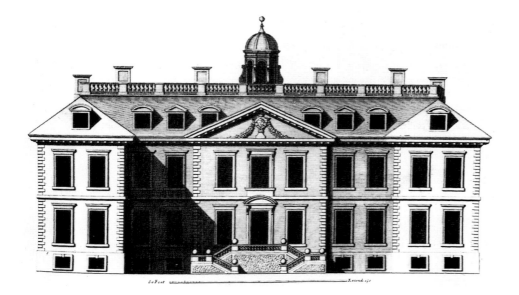

Rendering (by Colin Campbell) of Belton House, Lincolnshire

THE MOUNT

*Architectural drawings
(by Hoppin & Koen) of
west and east elevations
and (opposite)
north elevation and
longitudinal section*

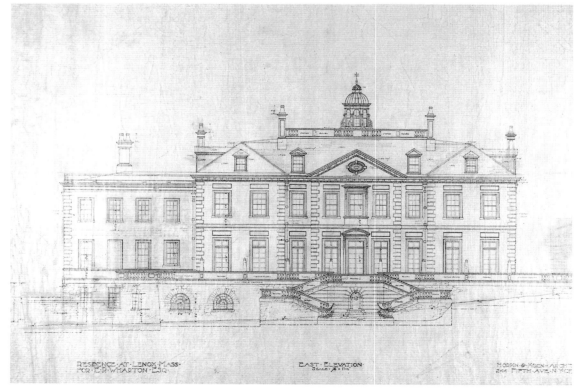

RESIDENCE·AT·LENOX·MASS·
FOR·E·R·WHARTON·ESQ·

NORTH·ELEVATION·
Scale ¼"=1'-0"

MOPPIN·&·KOEN·ARCH'TS
244·FIFTH·AVE·N·Y·CITY

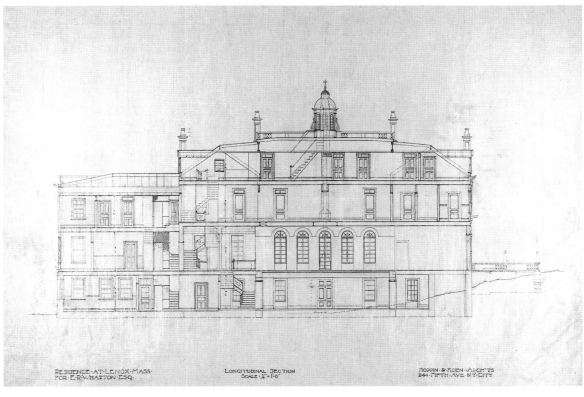

RESIDENCE·AT·LENOX·MASS·
FOR·E·R·WHARTON·ESQ·

LONGITUDINAL·SECTION
Scale ¼"=1'-0"

MOPPIN·&·KOEN·ARCH'TS
244·FIFTH·AVE·N·Y·CITY

stargazing, and perhaps most important, stimulating and amusing conversations with good friends, including Henry James, Walter Berry, and Beatrix Jones Farrand, among many others. Wharton expressed her devotion to the Berkshires in a letter to Bernard Berenson in 1911: "This place of ours is really beautiful; & the stillness, the greenness, the exuberance of my flowers, the perfume of my hemlock woods, & above all the moonlight nights on my big terrace, overlooking the lake, are a very satisfying change from six months of Paris."

INTERIORS

Like the exteriors, the interiors and gardens of The Mount display both varied influences and a graceful symmetry. The house is entered through the forecourt, which leads to a white marble stoop and vestibule. The vestibule has a spacious and airy feeling with an arched ceiling. Across the threshold was a statue of the god Pan in a grottolike niche containing a fountain. Terra-cotta tiles cover the floor of the vestibule and the floor molding is of Italian marble of green and black tones. The walls are painted stucco, and it was furnished with Italian marble benches and table. The vestibule provides a transition between the courtyard, which can be considered an outdoor room, and the stair hall. The door from the forecourt is wooden, and the door connecting the vestibule and stair hall has large panes of glass. The Mount's vestibule is in accordance with the principles of *The Decoration of Houses*. It forms a pleasing transition from the driveway and courtyard to the house and is constructed of sturdy, serviceable materials, as were its furnishings. The glass door opening onto the stair hall both admitted desired guests and excluded the unwelcome.

THE MOUNT

Ground-floor entrance vestibule ca. 1900–1910

The prominent feature of the stair hall is a French-style wooden staircase with a black-painted wrought-iron railing. The furnishings of the stair halls, like those in the vestibule, were marble tables and benches. The floor of the stair hall consists of contrasting hardwoods designed in hexagons with a border of hardwoods in three shades. The walls were painted a neutral color with matching solid carpeting on the stairs. The upper landing of the staircase, on the main floor, features two nineteenth-century paintings by an unknown artist, both depicting a group of three eighteenth-century French

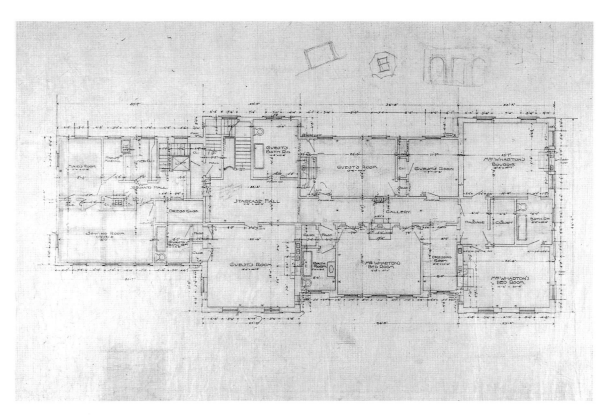

THE MOUNT

Floor plans (drawings by Hoppin & Koen)

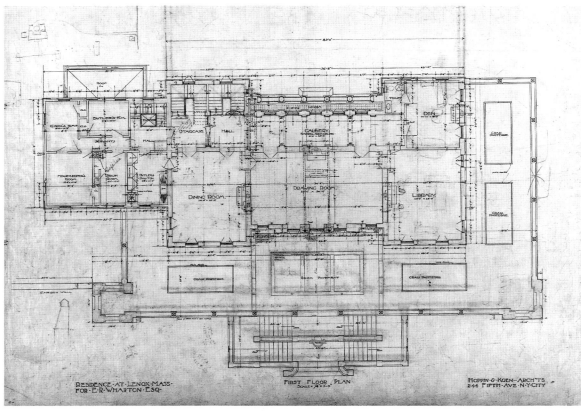

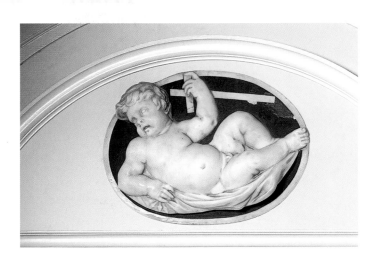

THE MOUNT

Main stair hall (opposite); plaster cherub in gallery, gallery toward den, gallery toward stair hall (during Wharton's ownership)

nobles. Above each painting is a decorative overpanel designed by Ogden Codman and executed in plaster. The overpanels harmoniously enhance the paintings with their pattern of leaves, flowers, and fruit. The decorative treatment of the staircase walls serves both aesthetic and informational purposes. As Scott Marshall notes: "The paintings serve as part of the transitional sequence from the outdoor into the mansion by illustrating garden scenes with elegantly dressed figures in French court dress. Before a visitor had actually entered the main body of the house, these figures introduced the motif of the interior appointments and furnishings (Louis XV and Louis XVI) of the Whartons."

At the staircase landing on the main floor are doors leading to the dining room, an open arch leading to the gallery, and closed glass double doors to the right to balance the open arch. The closed glass doors on the upper landing of the stair hall lead to the bedroom floor.

The gallery appears through the open arch and runs the length of the west facade to the den on the north. The gallery has a barrel-arched ceiling with eight arches. Three oversize windows on the west are balanced by an arch on the opposite wall flanked by arched doors to the drawing room. The chiefly terrazzo floor is bordered with a reddish-veined Italian marble, and the design of banded circles is accomplished with white Vermont marble. The banded-circle design is present in other parts of the mansion. The bas-relief of a child holding a cross over the threshold of the den, although it has religious overtones, surprisingly resembles the cupids used to decorate Edith Wharton's book of verse *Artemis to Actaeon and Other Verses* (1909).

The walls and ceiling of the gallery are constructed of plaster and wood and it was lighted by chandeliers. The gallery certainly meets the requirements set forth in *The Decoration of Houses* in its use of durable, beautiful Italian marble, dramatic vaulted-ceiling treatment, chandelier lighting, sparse elegant furnishings, and original statuary. Its floors particularly follow Wharton's preferences: "The inlaid marble floors of the Italian palaces, whether composed of square or diamond-shaped blocks, or decorated with a large design in different colors, are unsurpassed in beauty."

The threshold at the north end of the gallery leads through glass doors (one is false) to the den, once Teddy Wharton's place for relaxation. Though relatively small (roughly fourteen by eighteen feet), it has a French marble fireplace and two French doors leading to the wraparound terrace. The south side has two doors, one to the gallery and one to a bathroom. Ogden Codman designed ornamented wall panes for the den similar to those he designed for Land's End in Newport. The plasterwork medallion above the

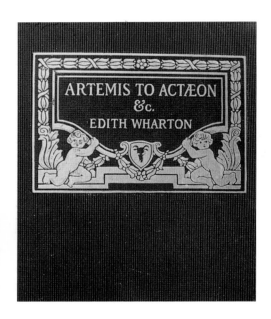

Book cover, Artemis to Actaeon and Other Verses, *first edition, 1909*

mirrored overmantel of the fireplace is similar to the medallion in his drawings for the library at Land's End. The fireplace is of French rouge marble with insets of Belgian black marble; it features an interesting cast-iron fireback. Four large wall panels are ornamented with beaded trim and a decorative border. The coved ceiling is joined to the walls by a detailed cornice. A concealed door—perhaps a sacrifice to the god of symmetry—joins the east wall of the den to the library. (Concealment was deemed necessary as there was no balancing door on the west wall.) The floor of the den is trellis-patterned oak parquet to match the floor in the library. As Teddy used the den to attend to the affairs of the estate or to relax, it was probably comfortably furnished according to the dictates of *The Decoration of Houses*, where Wharton and Codman write: "It is usually conceded that common sense should regulate the furnishing of the den."

THE MOUNT

Oak-paneled bookcases in the library ca. 1900–1910

The library can be accessed through the concealed door in the den and through a door on the east wall of the gallery. It was designed for Edith's use and privacy and also lent itself to an area where guests felt welcome to take tea, read, or converse. Four terrace doors with decorative Louis XV–style brass hardware (from the French firm Sterlin) open into the library. The library walls are paneled in oak with Codman-designed scrollwork and garlands. The north, south, and east walls have built-in oak bookcases. The walls ascend to a plaster cornice decorated with three motifs and then to a coved ceiling. There is evidence that Edith considered beautifully crafted volumes along with elegant bookcases to be the focus of attention in the library. As *The Decoration of Houses* states: "The general decoration of the library should be of such character as to form a background or setting to the books, rather than to distract attention from them. The richly adorned room in which books are but a minor incident is, in fact, no library at all." In regard to bookcases, it is noted that: "The French architect always preferred to build his bookshelves into niches formed in the thickness of the wall, thus utilizing the books as part of his scheme of decoration. There is no doubt that this is not only the most practical, but the most decorative, way of housing any collection of books large enough to be so employed."

Although Edith wrote in bed in the mornings, her library was used not only to contain her volumes but as a repository for her mail, new books, and current periodicals and as a cozy spot to entertain her friends around the

THE MOUNT

*View of the terrace
from the den, brass
library-door handle*

library fire. Her desk was of the *bureau-ministre* type described in *The Decoration of Houses*. It had a large surface and sides that came out to hold excess material. Her desk chair was a caned Louis XV–style one. Near her desk was a Louis XV *lit de repos*, and on one wall stood an ample table in the style of her desk.

The French green marble fireplace is close to the south wall and features French rouge marble insets. The decorative fireback displays a mythological scene. A portrait of Edith's great-grandfather Ebenezer Stevens hung over the mantel. The furniture around the hearth consisted of fringed armchairs flanking the fireplace and a settee facing the hearth. This comfortable corner of the library was the setting of Wharton's fondly remembered "reading around the library fire" with Henry James, Walter Berry, and Gaillard Lapsley, among others. The tables on each side of the fireplace may have accommodated the books needed for such readings. Both were Louis XV side tables and the round table had an inlaid surface and ormolu mounts. A tapestry in a garden motif hung on the west wall of the library. The area in front of the tapestry held another Louis XV marble-surfaced table and two small inlaid Louis XVI cabinets. A marble bust was placed on each of these tables.

THE MOUNT

*Library tapestry
ca. 1900–1910*

On the south wall of the library is a door leading to the drawing room, or formal salon. The drawing room can also be reached from double doors leading to the dining room on the south wall and three sets of double doors on the east wall leading to the terrace. The drawing room ceiling has an elaborate plaster ornamental scheme with a floral and fruit motif. The walls also have plaster ornamentation of flower garlands. The floor of the drawing room utilizes the same terrazzo and Vermont white marble as the gallery. The French marble fireplace, with three Italian marble insets and decorative fireback, is the most elaborate one at The Mount. The fireback is decorated with the biblical story of Abraham and Isaac in the central oval, which is surrounded by three cupids. The side panels depict the same scene. The interior doors of the drawing room are ornamented with broken pediments. The room probably had French furnishings that were elegant yet comfortable. This country drawing room most likely served as a formal salon, or *salon de compagnie*, and with its comfortable furnishings and access to the terrace, as an often-used room for the Whartons and their guests.

The double doors on the south wall of the drawing room connect it to the dining room. Symmetrical double doors on the south wall of the dining room open into the butler's pantry, and double doors on the east wall join the dining room to the terrace. The floor is terrazzo bordered with white marble. A two-tiered cornice joins the ceiling to the paneled stucco walls, which have plaster ornaments depicting fruit, vegetables, flowers, and fish. Within these ornaments are paintings. There are also plaster ornaments over the doors to the drawing room and pantry and over the two doors on the west wall. The painting framed by the plasterwork ornamentation on the south wall is a Flemish-style *nature morte*. The French rouge marble fireplace with insets of black Belgian marble features a cast-iron fireback depicting an unknown mythological or biblical scene. The painting over the fireplace depicts cupids, flowers, and fruit. The dining room furniture was moved to The Mount from Land's End and consisted of a pedestal extension dining table (a type not recommended in *The Decoration of Houses*), Louis XV–style white-painted cane chairs, a Louis XV–style china cabinet, and a decorative firescreen.

THE MOUNT

*Dining room
ca. 1900–1910*

The southernmost door on the west wall of the dining room leads to the stair hall to the bedroom floor; the northernmost door leads to the main stair hall. The two were separated to provide privacy for the inhabitants of the house. The stairs of the private staircase are painted wood and the walls have a simple molding. The railing is black-painted wrought iron. The landing of the stairs on the bedroom floor leads to an interior hallway running to the door of Edith Wharton's bedroom suite, on the north side of the house. The decoration of the hall is simple, with understated wall moldings and painted walls. On the west wall of the hall are doors to two guest rooms and one guest bath; the east wall has doors to Teddy Wharton's room, a bath, the Whartons' shared dressing room, and an additional guest room.

The east guest room is spacious, with plain plaster walls painted a light neutral color and a pine floor. It has an elegant French rouge marble fireplace and windows that had spectacular views of the terrace, meadow, lake, mountains, and walled garden. The guest bath for the east guest room is located just into the servants' area of the house at the south end of the hallway.

The west guest suite has two adjoining rooms, one perhaps a sitting room. The rooms are similar to the east guest room, with pine floors and painted walls. The fireplace in the larger room is of gray Baridiglio marble;

THE MOUNT

*Library desk and book-
cases, library with
doors to drawing room*

THE MOUNT

*Plaster medallion and
floral painting in Edith
Wharton's boudoir*

the door to the bathroom is on the south wall. The smaller room has a door to the main hallway. It is a small-scale version of the bedroom suite described in *The Decoration of Houses.*

Teddy Wharton's bedroom suite is entered by a door on the east side of the hall. It is located over the drawing room, and its east windows overlooked the parterres, gardens, pond, lake, and mountains. A fireplace of Spanish marble of black and white hues is on the west wall; the floor is of pine and the walls were painted. Teddy's bathroom has doors both from his bedroom and from the hallway, a practice recommended in *The Decoration of Houses* to afford privacy to the suite's inhabitants and to allow the servants easy access.

Edith Wharton's bedroom suite is at the northern end of the floor and consists of her bedroom, boudoir, bathroom, and the shared dressing room. The walls of her bedroom were a simple white and the floor is oak parquet. The French marble fireplace has gray and black tones. The room was lit by wall sconces. As Edith wrote in bed and mused about her creations, one of the features of this room that may have particularly pleased her is the north windows, which looked out on the terrace, rock garden, seasonal flowering

Red Garden, and the woodlands. The east windows gave views over the terrace to the rolling lawn, meadow, pond, and lake. Her suite's bathroom is between her bedroom and boudoir and is accessible to the servants by a door on the hall. Her boudoir occupies the northwest corner of the bedroom floor. The north windows are complemented by two windows on the west wall. Ogden Codman decorated the boudoir with eight paintings on floral themes in the Dutch style of the seventeenth century. The cornice has a pattern of acanthus leaves, and all four walls contain plaster medallions in a fruit and floral motif. The French rouge fireplace on the north wall has a decorative fireback depicting a mythological scene. Scott Marshall's research discovered that the furnishings of the boudoir included a *lit de repos* and a French-style desk and sofa. The curtains and sofa were done in the same fabric. In the use of similar fabric for curtains and furnishings and in the choice of furniture, the boudoir corresponded with the principles of *The Decoration of Houses* in that it was a "simple room, gay and graceful in decoration."

Although the design of servants' areas is not covered in *The Decoration of Houses,* life at The Mount could not be conducted in accordance with its creators' desires without a full complement of help. Servants in residence included a housekeeper, butler, housemaids, footmen, cook, kitchen help, and Edith's personal maid. The caretaker lived in the gatehouse, the coachman above the stable, and the chauffeur in a neighboring town. Nonresident gardeners, grooms, and laborers were also required. The resident household workers were to be found in the south wing of The Mount and the attic, areas given over to the staff. The basement floor of the service area comprised the kitchen, servants' dining room, serving area, laundry room, storage room, wine cellar, lamp room, and furnace and coal cellar. The service elevator goes from the basement to the main floor of The Mount. The service stairs start on the main floor and run to the attic. The first-floor service area contains the pantry, brush room, housekeeper's room, cook's room, and butler's room, all opening onto the servants' hall. When a bell rang, an indicator box in the hall displayed twelve locations where a servant might be needed.

The second floor of the service wing is divided into a maid's room, sewing room, dress closet, linen closet, housemaid's closet, and other closets. Edith Wharton's personal maid occupied the maid's room on this floor, a location that afforded her speedy access to Edith's bedroom suite. The attic floor of the service wing has eight servants' rooms and two bathrooms. The rooms have plaster walls, pine floors, dormer windows, and closets. The service wing was designed to accommodate the number and type of staff needed by the Whartons, and its design proved adequate to their needs.

THE MOUNT

Drawing room, nature morte *painting in dining room, fireback in drawing room fireplace, detail of plasterwork in dining room, detail of plasterwork in boudoir*

THE MOUNT

Red Garden (during Wharton's ownership) with trellis (designed by Ogden Codman Jr.)

GARDENS

Edith Wharton was the primary landscape and formal garden planner at The Mount but she was influenced by Ogden Codman, who had helped with her garden at Land's End in Newport; Francis Hoppin; and her niece Beatrix Jones Farrand. She had also been forming impressions of landscapes and gardens from her childhood in Europe and her subsequent travels there. She planned her garden at The Mount between 1903 and 1905 and spent the early months of 1904 traveling in Italy and writing articles for *Century* magazine, which titled her series *Italian Villas and Their Gardens*. The series appeared in book form in 1904.

The impressions Edith formed in Italy certainly played a part in the design of her own New England landscape. Beatrix Farrand designed the approach to the mansion, which Thomas S. Hayes details in an introductory essay to the reprint of *Italian Villas and Their Gardens:*

> The drive consists of three well-planned sections. The first from the front gate is an 800-foot sugar-maple allée with a succession of structures seen on the left: the lodge or estate superintendent's residence, the greenhouse, the double-cruciform kitchen garden, and the stable. For the second section, the drive curves through

THE MOUNT

*View from garden path
ca. 1900–1910*

the rugged terrain of wooded stony hillocks. A meandering brook follows its natural course, passing twice under the roadbed. The natural vegetation of oak, white pines, and maples with a lush groundcover of ferns and periwinkle planted by Edith Wharton hugs the edges of the road. The third section is the grand sweep of lawn and drive approaching the house.

The kitchen garden, also designed by Farrand, is no longer present at The Mount, but the other formal gardens are being restored. The outlines of three formal gardens are visible from the east terrace. The Red Garden was to the left; straight ahead were hemlock-bordered lawn terraces descending the hillside; and on the right was a walled garden. Between the Red Garden and the walled garden was a linden-bordered gravel walk.

The Red Garden was Edith's blooming garden. It had a formal design of rectangles within rectangles with a rectangular pool and dolphin fountain in the center. Paths divided one of the inner rectangles into L-shaped flower beds with topiary bushes. A trellised garden niche designed by Ogden Codman was transferred from Land's End to The Mount. Although Wharton did not rank flowers as a primary element in garden design, some of the varieties she planted are listed in a 1905 letter to Sara Norton:

THE MOUNT

*Garden plan (drawn
by Carole Palermo-
Schulze), view from
the Red Garden*

THE MOUNT

The Red Garden
fountain
ca. 1900–1910

It is really what I thought it never could be—a "mass of bloom." Ten varieties of phlox, some very gorgeous are flowering together, and then the snapdragons, lilac and crimson stocks, penstemons, annual pinks in every shade of rose, salmon, cherry and crimson, the lovely white physostegia, the white petunias— which now form a perfect hedge about the tank—the intense blue delphinium, the purple and white platycodon, etc.—really, with the background of hollyhocks of every shade, from pale rose to dark red, it looks for a fleeting moment, like a garden in some civilized climate.

The walled garden is a cross-shaped, cloisterlike *giardino segreto* with ten-foot rough stone walls on three sides enclosing an eighty-foot square. In the center are a fountain and a circular pool, which Edith bordered with petunias. The west wall, set against the hillside, serves as a retaining wall. The east wall opens to the surrounding meadow through six stone arches, three on each side, separated by stone pediments draped in grape vines. The view through the arches is of an expansive lawn and tall fir trees. The firs are now so tall that they obscure the Whartons' original view, which extended as far as the Berkshire Mountains. The south wall sports stone benches in stone niches. The north "wall" consists of a barrier of trees with a shaded path returning to the mansion itself. All moods could be accommodated in the *giardino segreto*. A visitor could commune with and be revitalized by nature, or sit on a bench and indulge in solitary meditation while listening to the

THE MOUNT

*The central fountain
of the walled garden
ca. 1900–1910*

soothing water flow of the fountain. Thus refreshed, a guest could slowly walk up the stone path and return to the companionship of the Whartons or other visitors at The Mount. The terrace, which had obelisks and statues, is part of the grounds as well as part of the house. In sum, the gardens have a harmonious balance of what Edith recommends in *Italian Villas and Their Gardens*—marble, water, and "perennial verdure."

LITERARY ACTIVITY

The years at The Mount were productive ones for Wharton. She completed *Italian Villas and Their Gardens* (1904); the travelogues *Italian Backgrounds* (1905) and *A Motor-Flight Through France* (1908); the novellas *Sanctuary* (1903) and *Madame de Treymes* (1907); a book of verse, *Artemis to Actaeon and Other Verses* (1909); and the short story collections *The Descent of Man and Other Stories* (1904), *The Hermit and the Wild Woman and Other Stories* (1908), and *Tales of Men and Ghosts* (1910). She finished her best-selling novel *The House of Mirth* (1905) as well as *The Fruit of the Tree* (1907). Edith may have written parts of *Ethan Frome* (1911) during this time, and she did early work on *The Custom of the Country* (1913).

THE MOUNT

The walled garden: fountain, steps to meadow,
south wall, steps to terrace, stone arches on east wall

Her literary work influenced her life at The Mount, from planning the landscape, gardens, and interior decoration to her tasks as a busy, gracious hostess. Her life at The Mount, in turn, influenced her writing. The planning of her gardens coincided with the writing of *Italian Villas and Their Gardens.* For the travelogue *Italian Backgrounds,* she visited various sections of Italy and was influenced by her impressions of the countryside and architecture. In the chapter "The Sanctuaries of the Pennine Alps," she describes visiting a location similar to The Mount's physical setting. She writes of a small lake, somewhat like Laurel Lake in character, near the town of Varallo: "From Varallo the fortunate traveller may carry his impressions unimpaired through the chestnut-woods and across the hills to the lake of Orta—a small sheet of water enclosed in richest verdure . . . The lake itself is begirt by vine-clad slopes, and in every direction roads and bridle-paths lead across the wooded primroses and lilies-of-the valley, to the deeper forest-recesses at the foot of the high Alps."

Research for *A Motor-Flight Through France* took her to many regions of that country and deepened her appreciation of its landscape and architecture. The volume views France and its feudal history in contrast with America and its desire for the new. Wharton found much to admire in the French countryside, cathedrals, and châteaus. She was exceedingly sensitive to the environment and often anthropomorphizes structures, such as the cathedral at Amiens:

> A great Gothic cathedral sums up so much of history, it has cost so much in faith and toil, in blood and folly and saintly abnegation, it has sheltered a long succession of lives, given collective voice to so many inarticulate and contradictory cravings, seen so much that was sublime and terrible, or foolish, pitiful and grotesque, that it is like some mysteriously preserved ancestor of the human race.

She also endowed Nohant, the country estate of George Sand, with the ability to exercise a stabilizing influence on the bohemians who lived and visited there and the local farmers who worked in its shadow. Wharton had expected that the mansion might have a shabby air about it but discovered that "One beholds this image of aristocratic well-being, this sober edifice, conscious in every line of its place in the social scale, of its obligations to the church and cottages under its wing, its rights over the acres surrounding it." She also viewed the beauties of the countryside as architectural. In describing Provence she writes: "Here was Provence at last—dry, clear-edged, classic— with a sky like blue marble, low red hills tufted by olives, stony hollows with thin threads of stream."

Her novella *Sanctuary* is partially set at a country estate surprisingly

She had meant to wait for him on the Terrace.

Frontispiece illustration, Sanctuary, *first edition, 1903; illustrations (opposite),* The Fruit of the Tree, Scribner's *magazine, spring 1907*

like The Mount. Kate Orme is reviewing her wedding invitations at her fiancé's country home; this is the scene in the drawing room:

> The large coolness of the room, its fine traditional air of spacious living, its out-look over field and woodland toward the lake lying under the silver bloom of September; the very scent of the late violets in a glass on the writing-table; the rosy-mauve masses of hydrangea in tubs along the terrace; the fall, now and then, of a leaf through the still air, all, somehow, were mingled in the suffusion of well-being that yet made them seem but so much dross upon its current.

The lake in this description will be the setting for a tragic accident. Incidentally, in developing the character of Kate's son, who hopes to become an architect, Wharton demonstrates her familiarity with the jargon of architecture and her knowledge of the neoclassical styles of early-twentieth-century civic institutions.

Madame de Treymes takes place primarily in Paris. In the novella, New York life is compared unfavorably to Parisian life. The short novel *Ethan Frome* is set near Lenox, Massachusetts, among the local farmers and merchants in the fictitious town of Starkfield, which is used as a metaphor for the physical and emotional isolation of the characters. Starkfield is described in winter: "Day by day, after the December snows were over, a blazing blue sky poured down torrents of light and air on the white landscape, which gave them back in an intense glitter. One would have supposed that such an atmosphere must quicken the emotions as well as the blood; but it seemed to produce no change except that of retarding still more the sluggish pulse of Starkfield." *The Fruit of the Tree* also has a Massachusetts setting in a mill town similar to North Adams.

The House of Mirth's locales are primarily fashionable New York at the turn of the century, Hudson Valley villas, and Europe, while *The Custom of the Country* is set chiefly in Old New York society during the first decade of the twentieth century and in Europe, particularly France. As in *A Motor-Flight Through France*, Wharton used *Custom* to comment on European ties to history and American affinity for and devotion to the new, on European interest in civilization and culture and American interest in business and finance.

Wharton's short stories of this time have diverse settings, including the drawing rooms, vestibules, libraries, studios, bedrooms, and men's clubs of fashionable New York society as well as Central Park, the Metropolitan Museum, and Brooklyn. Other American locales include fictitious cities in the Midwest, the summer resorts of Maine, and the mansions of the Hudson Valley. Among European locations are the English countryside, the Riviera, Venice, Florence, St. Cloud, and the Faubourg St. Germain.

Drawn by Alonzo Kimball. Half-way up the slope to the house they met.—Page 262.

Drawn by Alonzo Kimball. "IF ANYTHING GOES WRONG WITH THEM, IT'S JUST AS IF IT HAD GONE WRONG WITH

ENTERTAINING AT THE MOUNT

The Mount was designed for both privacy and company. In addition to producing a number of major works, Edith Wharton was a busy hostess there. She wrote in bed every morning and came down about noon for a solitary walk or companionable chat or stroll with one of her guests. Guests could enjoy outdoor activities, including golf, boating, and tennis. They also made the sociable round of picnics and dinners and enjoyed the diversion of walking or driving around the countryside. In her memoir Edith notes taking "long happy rides and drives through the wooded lanes of that loveliest region."

The years at The Mount were Edith's time for important growth both personally and professionally. Many of her guests remained loving and stalwart friends. The Mount provided her with a place to offer her hospitality and deepen her relationships with Henry James, Walter Berry, Gaillard Lapsley, John Hugh Smith, and Robert Norton, among others. Reports from Edith's frequent guests found The Mount perfectly comfortable and their host and hostess extremely congenial. Although Edith spent only about a decade in possession of The Mount before she decided to live in France, she remembered it fondly in *A Backward Glance*, where she wrote: "Its blessed influence still lives in me."

THE MOUNT

View at night

THE SALE OF THE MOUNT

Edith sailed for Europe in late October 1908; her love affair with American journalist Morton Fullerton may have then been at its height. Her years at The Mount were coming to a close. Edith moved into an apartment in Paris at 53, rue de Varenne in January 1910; the sale of the houses at 882 and 884 Park Avenue was imminent. The Whartons sold The Mount for any number of complicated reasons, but prominent among them were the mounting problems in Edith and Teddy's marriage. Their union, never really solid, was rapidly unraveling due to Teddy's various illnesses and Wharton's greater emotional independence. The Mount was rented in the summer of 1909, and neither Teddy nor Edith spent much time there afterward. As it was not practical to incur the large expense of maintaining the estate, the Whartons sold it in January 1912 to its 1909 summer tenants, Albert and Mary Shattuck. The sale of The Mount represented for Edith Wharton the severing of her major tie to the United States and signaled her permanent move to France, her adopted country.

She was simply one particular facet of the solid, glittering impenetrable body (Page 60)

The Faubourg
St. Germain
1907–1919

As the first decade of the century drew to a close, Edith Wharton found herself spending less time in New York and more time in Europe, especially France. Through the introductions of French friends, she had met many congenial Parisians who appreciated her literary work and with whom she felt comfortable discussing the artistic views of the period. A subtle shift in her desire to spend more time in Paris was evident.

Frontispiece illustration, Madame de Treymes, *first edition, 1907*

EXTENDED VISITS

In March 1906 Edith and Teddy sailed to Europe and rented a suite at the Hotel Domenici on rue Castiglione in Paris. The best-selling *House of Mirth* had established Edith as a serious writer and gave her an entrée into intellectual circles in the Faubourg St. Germain. The Whartons were reunited with the Bourgets, and novelist Paul Bourget introduced them to his friends and colleagues in the Parisian intellectual world. He also found a translator for *The House of Mirth:* Charles du Bos, a friend of André Gide. Edith's Parisian circle of friends came from various groups. As she recalls in her memoir: "My new friends came from worlds as widely different as the University, the literary and Academic milieux, and the old and aloof society of the Faubourg Saint Germain." Bourget introduced her to prominent members of all three groups, including the novelist and poet Comtesse Anna de Noailles, Comtesse Charlotte de Cossé-Brissac, the Byzantine historian Gustave Schlumberger, and the Parisian hostess Comtesse Rosa de Fitz-James, who through her salons introduced Edith to many other stimulating Parisians.

*3, place des Etats-Unis;
plaque honoring Edith
Wharton; 58, rue de
Varenne, housing the
George Vanderbilt
apartment*

EDITH WHARTON
1862 – 1937
ECRIVAIN AMERICAIN
PREMIERE FEMME DE LETTRES
A RECEVOIR
LE PRIX PULITZER (1921)
SEJOURNA DANS CETTE MAISON

Place de la Concorde

In her novella *Madame de Treymes,* written both in Paris and at The Mount, Wharton chronicles the married life of the American-born Marquise de Malrive, whose personality must be subdued in order for her to take her place beside her husband in the society of the French aristocracy. The recurrent theme of marriage as prison is present in this novel, but also present is an insight into Wharton's feelings about life in France, through the character John Durham:

> His European visits were infrequent enough to have kept unimpaired the freshness of his eye, and he was always struck by the vast and consummately ordered spectacle of Paris; by its look of having been boldly and deliberately planned as a background for the enjoyment of life, instead of being forced into grudging concessions to the festive instincts, or barricading itself against them in unenlightened ugliness, like his own lamentable New York.

In April 1906 the Whartons took up residence in the townhouse of Edith's brother Harry at 3, place des Etats-Unis, and Edith, feeling that Paris was particularly well suited to her emotional and intellectual needs, decided to search for a part-year residence there. In June 1906 the Whartons returned to The Mount for their usual summer and early fall activities, but January 1907 found them again crossing the Atlantic for the pleasant atmosphere of Paris. They had arranged to rent the Faubourg St. Germain apartment of the George Vanderbilts, located in a Louis XIV townhouse in the seventh arrondissement at 58, rue de Varenne, which R. W. B. Lewis describes as "one of the more luxurious apartments in the city—six or seven rooms, a kitchen and pantry, and two baths." Edith demonstrates her satisfaction with the apartment in a letter to her friend Sara Norton, reported in Lewis' *Edith Wharton:* "This very beautiful apartment, with charming old furniture, old Chinese porcelains and fine bronzes, against an harmonious background of real old *boiseries* (the hotel was built in 1720), [is] in the heart of the most delightful part of Paris." The Whartons rented this apartment again for the 1908–9 season. The lease ran out in April 1909, and Alice (Mrs. Cornelius) Vanderbilt was scheduled to take it over. Edith then transferred her household to an elegant suite at the Hôtel Crillon on the place de la Concorde, an environment she found dignified and suited to her needs and offering the type of elegant surroundings she often contrasted with the unsuitable, glamorous Ritz Hotel, which opened in 1898. She demonstrated her pleasure with these surroundings by spending the entire year of 1909 in France or Europe.

Wharton's extended stays in Paris during the years 1907–9 placed her in a particular moment in French cultural history—the midst of the belle époque, the period starting roughly at the turn of the century and ending with the outbreak of World War I. Americans were visiting Paris in record numbers and staying for longer periods. Belle-époque Paris offered a glamorous social life for wealthy Americans and serious cultural pursuits for those so inclined. Because of her social standing and wealth, Edith was involved in various social activities common to Americans of her class, and due to her literary pursuits and knowledge of many academic subjects, she sought out intellectual companionship. She often attended the salon of Comtesse Rosa de Fitz-James, where diplomats, scholars, writers, and intellectuals mingled. Its participants included members of the French aristocracy, such as Comte d'Haussonville (grandson and biographer of Madame de Staël), the historian Comte Henri de Segur, and the scholar Baron Ernest Seillière. Other salon guests included Charles du Bos; Anna de Noailles; playwrights Paul Hervieu and Marquis de Flers; Morton Fullerton; Gustave Schlumberger; the painter Jacques-Emile Blanche; the pastor of Ste. Clothilde, Abbé Mugnier; the poet and novelist Henri de Regnier; and of course, Paul Bourget. This salon represented a commingling of the society Edith Wharton frequented in Paris.

The salon life of the aristocracy in such settings as Madame de Fitz-James' drawing room is the subject of Marcel Proust's compelling novels. Ever observant of her surroundings, Wharton, in *A Backward Glance,* presents an insight into the salon and its hostess by describing the townhouse rooms where the gathering took place:

Hôtel Crillon:
facade, lobby,
marble entrance
hall

The salon in question looked out on the mossy turf and trees of an eighteenth-century *hôtel* standing between court and garden in the Rue de Grenelle. A few years later it was transferred to a modern building in the Place des Invalides . . . The three drawing-rooms, which opened into one another, were as commonplace as rooms can be in which every piece of furniture, every picture and every ornament is in itself a beautiful thing, yet the whole reveals no trace of the owner's personality. In the first drawing-room, a small room hung with red damask, Madame de Fitz-James . . . received her intimates. Beyond was the big drawing-room, with pictures by Ingres and David on the pale walls, and tapestry sofas and arm-chairs; it was there that the dinner guests assembled. Opening out of it was another small room, lined with ornate Louis XV bookcases in which rows of rare books in precious bindings stood in undisturbed order—for Madame de Fitz-James was a book-collector, not a reader.

Mindful of the lack of intellectual curiosity in Madame de Fitz-James, Edith nevertheless appreciated her capability as a hostess who could bring together a stimulating mix of guests in a gracious setting. Wharton's continued rapture with France is apparent when, in her memoir, she contrasts the French salon with American dinner parties: "The whole *raison d'être* of the French *salon* is based on the national taste for general conversation. The two-and-two talks which cut up Anglo-Saxon dinners, and isolate guests at table and in the drawing-room, would be considered not only stupid but ill-bred in a society where social intercourse is a perpetual exchange, a market to which every one is expected to bring his best for barter."

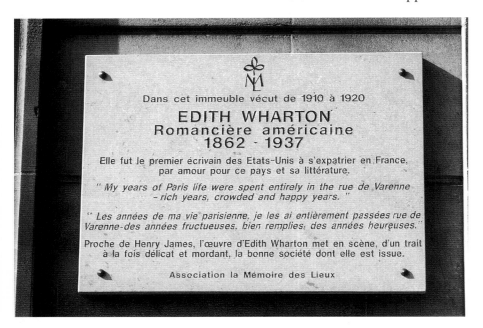

Plaque honoring Edith Wharton at 53, rue de Varenne

Madame de Fitz-James' salon represented a mixture of established French society, sprinkled with diplomats, academicians, writers, and painters; Edith also attended a salon centered around Jacques-Emile Blanche and other artists and writers. She felt fortunate to be a member of this group, which, as she recalls fondly and descriptively,

met on Sundays in the delightful informality of his studio, or about a tea-table under the spreading trees of the garden. The lofty studio-living-room . . . was in those days the most perfect setting for such meetings. Everything in it was harmonious in colour and tone, from the tall Coromandel screen, the old Chinese rugs on the floor, and the early Chinese bronzes and monochrome porcelains, to the crowning glory of the walls hung with pictures by Renoir, Degas, Manet, Corot, Boudin, Alfred Stevens and Whistler—the "Bathing Women" of Renoir, the sombre and powerful "Young Woman with the Glove" of Manet . . . or else in the upper gallery, some of the most notable of our host's own portraits, the perfect study of Thomas Hardy, the Degas, the Debussy, the Aubrey Beardsley, the George Moore and the young Marcel Proust.

In this stimulating setting the guests included Diaghilev, the playwright Henry Bernstein, George Moore, André Gide, and the painters Walter Sickert and Ricketts. On other afternoons a group of music lovers met at the Blanches "to listen to Bach and Beethoven, Franck, Debussy or Chauson, with those great pictures looking down from the walls, and the glimpse of lawn and shady trees deepening the impression of the music by enclosing it in a country solitude." Edith was also introduced to the young Jean Cocteau at the Blanches' summer home in Offranville, and Cocteau made many subsequent visits to Edith on rue de Varenne.

Edith's new acquaintances were complemented by the personal circle of friends that spent time with her in Paris: Henry James, Walter Berry, Bernard Berenson, and her lover, Morton Fullerton. Old and new friends provided Edith with a stimulating and appealing atmosphere in belle-époque Paris and probably influenced her decision to find a permanent home there.

53, RUE DE VARENNE

When the lease on 58, rue de Varenne was up in April 1909, Edith's brother Harry found a suitable apartment for the Whartons across the street at 53, rue de Varenne near the rue du Bac, and Edith moved there in January 1910. On January 23 a major flood swept through Paris. Inexplicably, Edith's portion of the rue de Varenne did not suffer severe damage, although much of the seventh arrondissement was inundated. R. W. B. Lewis in *Edith Wharton* reports: "The river

Rue du Bac, before and during the 1910 flood

waters poured down Rue Vaneau into Rue Bellechasse; to the right, the Rue du Bac was transformed into a lake, with wooden bridges hastily erected for pedestrians to cross it." Flood relief efforts dominated Paris for several months, but when the danger was over Edith could settle into her new home, which Lewis describes:

53, RUE DE VARENNE

Street facade; courtyard door; Edith Wharton in courtyard, 1914

Luxembourg Gardens

The apartment had a series of balconies giving onto the street, but the interior was designed to face away from the traffic and to look down onto the privacy of a large courtyard; next to it were the attractive Cité de Varenne (a small enclosed residential area which the English would call a close) and the gardens of the Doudeauville *hôtel* . . . In addition to the library, the spacious, high-ceilinged drawing room, the elegant dining room (all in a row above the court), and a good-sized kitchen and pantry, there were half a dozen bedrooms of various sizes, another sitting room . . . and several inadequately equipped bathrooms. The apartment contained what amounted to a guest suite; a bedroom and bath, and for private access a back stairs leading down to the courtyard.

Unfortunately no photographs showing the interior of this apartment have come to light.

With her new home, Edith could settle into the seventh arrondissement and enjoy the pleasures of the Faubourg St. Germain. In *A Backward Glance,* she recalls the decision to leave the New York townhouse for the spacious Parisian apartment: "A year or two after the publication of 'The House of Mirth' my husband and I decided to exchange our little house in New York for a flat in Paris . . . A house and garden of my own, anywhere on the coast between Marseilles and Frejus, would have made me happy; since that could not be, my preference was for a flat in Paris, where I could see people who shared my tastes." As a fledgling yet successful author, Wharton found the French appreciation for literature deeply supportive and perhaps comforting. She recalled: "In Paris no one could live without literature, and the fact that I was a professional writer, instead of frightening my fashionable friends, interested them."

Wharton found the faubourg, with its elegant, classical architecture, relative tranquillity, and proximity to cultural events, the best of several worlds. Her new surroundings in the seventh arrondissement are aptly described by R. W. B. Lewis: "The town seat of the most imposing of the French nobility; an aristocratic society slowly being penetrated by bourgeois artists and intellectuals; the standard of social behavior for the other faubourgs in Paris; an atmosphere, a cluster of traditions." Both the poet Rainer Maria Rilke and the sculptor Rodin resided on rue de Varenne.

Painting, sculpture, literature, music, and drama were flourishing and being discussed animatedly in the more intellectual salons of the faubourg. The booksellers in the shops and along the quais enjoyed a brisk business, and the cosmopolitan inhabitants of Paris could enjoy a stroll in both the formal garden areas and the shady garden paths of the tranquil Luxembourg Gardens. More glamorous pursuits could also be enjoyed. In *The Belle Epoque* Hebe Dorsey presents a glimpse of the social and artistic whirl of Paris at that time:

> The Belle Epoque is associated with Paris at its most frolicsome . . . and, in counterpoint with an innocent milieu in which pretty debutantes played croquet on summer lawns and sailor-suited children went to the rond-point des Champs-Elysées with beribboned nurses. In this carefree society, privileged people had everything they could ask for, including that most precious of today's commodities—time. To strains of Offenbach, they went from balls to receptions, and from spas to châteaux. Belle Epoque also conjures up society women strolling in the Bois de Boulogne, and salons filled with elegant mustachioed men . . . Arts were important and the Belle Epoque was a golden age for music, theatre and visual arts, superbly represented by such people as Verdi and Puccini, Ravel, and Massenet, Tolstoy and D'Annunzio, Sarah Bernhardt and Eleonora Duse, and the Impressionist masters Monet and Manet. The period closed with the explosive, brilliant Ballets Russes.

Wharton, although not a frivolous person, certainly availed herself of the cultural advantages of the belle époque. Through Jacques-Emile Blanche she became more acquainted with artists and composers of the period. She met Diaghilev at Madame de Fitz-James' salon and attended performances of the Ballets Russes, which she termed "the last vision of beauty before the war." She was also particularly taken with the modern dance of Isadora Duncan, whose performance at the Paris Opéra she attended. She reports that in Duncan's performance: "I beheld the dance I had always dreamed of, a flowing of movement into movement, an endless interweaving of motion and music, satisfying every sense as a flower does, or a phrase of Mozart's." She was also deeply impressed with Proust's *Du coté de chez Swann:* "I began to read languidly, felt myself, after two pages, in the hands of a master, and was presently trembling with the excitement which only genius can communicate."

Luxembourg Gardens:
flowerbeds in front of the
Palais du Luxembourg,
tree-lined path

SOCIAL LIFE AT NEWPORT.

Bevy of Handsome Girls Who Will Be Prominent in New York This Winter.

YOUNG MR. HENRY CLEWS' FAD.

He Creates a Mild Sensation by Wearing White Silk Socks at a Dance.

[From the NEW YORK HERALD.]

NEW YORK, Sunday.—There will be a bevy of handsome girls in society this coming winter, some of whom have been "half" out either at the opera or small dances. The Newport contingent, now very much in evidence, will come in for a good share of attention. Among these are Miss Laura Swan, Mrs. Elisha Dyer's daughter; Miss Sallie Van Alen, whose resemblance to Cléo de Mérode is frequently alluded to; Miss Marion Fish, who rides a good deal with her mother; Miss Fanny Jones, for whom a good many parties are being given, and Miss Evelyn Blight.

Possibly to this list may be added the Misses Mills, who are likely to be seen occasionally in society during the winter, although they will probably not be formally introduced.

All these mentioned may be classed among the athletic girls of society, for they seem to live in the open air, golfing, swimming, riding or playing tennis. The Misses Mills have already distinguished themselves as golf champions, and they will figure at the coming horse show in several classes. They drive extremely well, and no doubt will carry off some of the prizes.

A singular feature of summer life, especially where the automobile is extensively used, is the absolute fearlessness displayed by the women. It is a remarkable sight, to say the least, to see two or three elegantly dressed women, without maid or groom, speeding to or from a dinner in one of the elegantly appointed "bubbles" that are so much favored. This is a common sight, especially at Newport, more often in midweek, when the husbands are away at business. But Newport has such excellent roads that there is no apparent danger, and women are decidedly expert in running the machines.

Milk White Socks.

Young Henry Clews, Jr., has set a fashion decidedly noticeable, but probably not to be widely followed. The other night he appeared at a dance with milk-white socks—silk, of course—which, in contrast to his black pumps and evening dress, made him the butt of kindly merriment. The colors of socks have run the entire gamut of shades, and even a screaming scarlet or the palest blue might escape without comment, but white, never.

Mr. Clews, Jr., does not confine himself to the wearing of white socks in the evening, but in the day time as well this part of his attire is noticeable. When running his "bubble" he has a fashion of throwing one leg over the other so that one foot rests on the other knee, thus displaying an expanse of pure white footgear. Thus it is that extremities set the fashion—red-headed women and white-socked men.

port as the guest of Dr. and Mrs. John H. French.

Mr. and Mrs. Joseph Harriman ... to have Mr. and ... Herbe... as their guests ... Whether Dr. and Mrs. a while longer dinner Sunday or all appeared Mrs. Scott skating park Henry Bowen French and ... ntinued M. Ec-Mr. Barto... nt, is not thick port to spend time ... tres as yet.

Mrs. C. A ... orning if there ... ightful dinner has been keep—

For the first count of the ... and Mrs. Lu ... ho know what part, the guest all inquires, R. Bishop, who ... there is to Theodore Have ... Bellevue avenue, the park formally intrud ... by an eager daughter to s ... id: "Ma foi! ... anged to sa ... w how the ice ... tain to New Yo ... is only three

Mr. and Miss thick, but if have found the ... here the park nished home, ... te glanced at Fifth avenue ... ber keeps on cool and comfort ... enough by in town all su ... ne ice must be for Europe ... hock to allow of propose to mak ... people skat— France, Germa ... on that if it may not return ... ght, which is until next Febru ... ty of skaters

No date has ... he end of the wedding of Mis ... of Mr. and Mr—Mr. Langdon B ... **BAMP.**
Mr. and Mrs. H ... living at La engagement was ... cy, Seine-et-ago. ...

Engagements /stmas night,

Several inter ... man was dis-announced last ... house by a the information ... been ... -daughter of Dr. ... He made his fin, and half-sis ... the "Temps," varro, former ... to the autho-American stag ... gagement to ... **PARIS.** well-known por ... of Professor ... tinguished p ... de Nuit, Griffin, who ... ut a thousand has made he ... ons in Paris, ap-last ten year ... cast-off cloth-well known in ... he most needy though an Amu ... refuges on all his life in L ... some apartment ... essed to the Lowndes squ ... ages at the fol-year ago last ... de Tocqueville, a reception ... oulevard de Cha-sion he was o ... f the Seine, and and Miss Ma ... on the south will be celeb—

Announcem ... tch any gifts gagement of ... contributions daughter of ... received. Pomeroy, of N ... Jenkins, of Sta ... roy, who has n ... sented, is an att ... favorite. The da ... not yet been deci—

Mr. and Mrs. J ... West 126th street, ment of their daugh ... ta Crandell, to Dr ... prominent physicia ... Miss Crandell com ... cestry, her paterna ... tors having been a ... in the Rhode Isla ... colonies. Dr. K ... this city, and afte ... ther course at t ... burgh. He is a m ... tive medical socie ... Westchester count ...

"Is there any skating?" exclaimed M. Eckart, secretary of the Cercle des Pa-

culars of a serious stabbing case at Charenton:—

A working cooper, named Louis Mar— on his way to his work at the ...int-Bernard, was attacked in ...aris by two men. One of them ...s, while the other stabbed him ...tween the shoulders. The un— ...an fell to the ground uncon— ...kmen who were passing sug—resting one of the assailants. ... his name as Ernest Cloin, a cooper, ... stated that his reason for stabbing Marchand was that the latter was courting his wife.

IN MEMORY OF THACKERAY.

Saturday being the thirty-fifth anniversary of the death of William Makepeace Thackeray, his bust in Poets' Corner, Westminster Abbey, was decked with a number of floral wreaths. The grave of Charles Dickens, situated almost below the bust of Thackeray, was also decorated with floral tributes.—Observer.

---

of a nature to call for investigation by the press."

The "Figaro" publishes this morning a more detailed contradiction which M. Bard has made through the Havas agency. The only communication which he had with Lieut.-Colonel Picquart was to inform him one day, at the request of the president of the Court, that he could not be heard on that day, and this was in the presence of the two gendarmes in whose custody he was. M. Bard adds that he has only broken through his rule of ignoring misstatements because the polite note which he sent to the "Temps" was published by that paper and might have been taken for an unsatisfactory rectification.

M. ESTERHAZY'S THREAT.

How He Is Said to Have Secured Col. von Schwartzkoppen's Silence.

The following statement, which, if true, tends to prove the relations existing between Major Esterhazy and Colonel von

---

NEW REVISION OF THE FOUR HUNDRED.

Mrs. John King Van Rensselaer Is Bringing Out a Series of Books on Old New York Families Which She Intends to Be a Guide to Social Rank.

MANY WELL KNOWN NAMES ARE OMITTED.

[From the NEW YORK HERALD.]

Mrs. John King Van Rensselaer, in order to establish clearly the identity of the descendants of New York's early settlers and those who have married into their families, has compiled an elaborate work, entitled "New Yorkers of the Nineteenth Century." This work, it is announced in the prospectus, "will be the standard of rank in New York," that it, it is intended to show what families were prominent here in the days of "old New York," or Man-ha-ta.

According to Mrs. Van Rensselaer, the originally prominent New York families are now represented, in descendants or membership by marriage, by about seven hundred families or about 3,500 individuals, although she confines her list in the first book of the series to the descendants of these twenty families:—

BARD,	JAY,
BARCLAY,	KING,
BRONSON,	LYNCH,
BUCHANAN,	McVICKAR,
DELAFIELD,	MORTON,
DUER,	RENWICK,
EMMET,	RUTHERFORD,
FISH,	SCHUYLER,
GLOVER,	STUYVESANT,
HOFFMAN,	VAN RENSSELAER

Other books which are to follow will include one hundred other families, the total

of 120 households, representing New York society of seventy years ago.

There are exactly 689 households, Mrs. Van Rensselaer finds, which are entitled to places in this genealogical record. As only "old New York" families are dealt with, from her list are missing the names of many New Yorkers included by Ward McAllister in the "Four Hundred." She does not include the Astors, Bloodgoods, Whitneys, Morgans, Winans or Goulds, and Mr. George Vanderbilt is the only member of that family included in the work. He owes this to his recent marriage to Miss Edith S. Dresser, who is of an old New York family.

For the same reason barely a dozen of those present at the first assembly in the Waldorf-Astoria on Thursday evening are referred to in her book by Mrs. Van Rensselaer. Neither Mr. Worthington Whitehouse, nor Mrs. Almeric Hugh Paget, who led the cotillon on that occasion, is mentioned.

Mrs. Van Rensselaer's latest book, which is handsomely printed on Dutch handmade linen paper, with binding of an old Dutch style, is designed to be the foremost genealogical record of its kind, and is expected to take the place here as to local families, that is filled by England's Burke's "Peerage, Baronetage and Landed Gentry."

AUTO SPEED IN NEW YORK.

[BY COMMERCIAL CABLE TO THE HERALD.]

NEW YORK, Saturday.—The discussion as to what is the "proper" speed for an automobile in this city continues. The aldermen threaten to pass an ordinance which will establish a ridiculously slow maximum.

In the meantime, however, an agreement has been made whereby some of the prominent "chauffeurs" are to take the aldermen out riding and give them a practical demonstration. The Tammany braves will be whisked over the park roads and ... the ease and safety with which ... handled.

TO AMERICANS VISITING LONDON.

The directors of the GOLDSMITHS' AND SILVERSMITHS' COMPANY, 112 REGENT-STREET, invite Americans to pay a visit to their store, which contains a most interesting collection of Diamond and Gem Work, Jewelry and Silver Plate. Should a purchase be contemplated, it will be found that the prices are from 25 to 50 per cent below those charged by other houses, as the company are manufacturers and supply persons, direct, thus saving all intermediate profits. The import duty will also be saved on articles purchased for personal use. Each article is marked in plain figures, a fixed net cash price. The company's exhibit at Chicago obtained not only the highest awards, but a special award was ... superiority of the exhibit.

Wharton's literary output between 1906 and 1910 reflected her new European life. Along with the comparisons between America and France in *Madame de Treymes*, other concerns were demonstrated in her two collections of short stories *The Hermit and the Wild Woman and Other Stories* (1908) and *Tales of Men and Ghosts* (1910), both of which she also worked on at The Mount. The short story "The Last Asset" takes place in the Faubourg St. Germain during the belle époque and concerns the relationships between Americans abroad and members of the French aristocracy. The rather déclassé Mrs. Sam Newell and her innocent daughter are residing at the ostentatious Ritz Hotel. Mrs. Newell has fallen on hard financial times and must try to marry the young Hermione to an affable French aristocrat. Mr. Newell has long lived apart from his wife and is currently residing in the faubourg; his presence is required at the wedding to satisfy the requirements of the groom's upright family. Mrs. Newell enlists Mr. Garnett, a fellow American, to persuade Mr. Newell to attend his daughter's wedding. In the course of the tale, the Ritz and the social pages of the Paris edition of the *New York Herald* are satirized. The clash of nouveau-riche American mores with the customs of upper-crust French society is apparent.

Society page, New York Herald *(Paris edition),* 1902

Wharton's vivid descriptions of the characters' surroundings serve to elucidate their personalities. Mrs. Newell's sitting room illustrates her penchant for style over substance: "Her sitting-room at Ritz's was full of warmth and fragrance. Long-stemmed roses filled the vases on the chimney-piece, in which a fire sparkled with that effect of luxury which fires produce when the weather is not cold enough to justify them." Mr. Newell's character is epitomized by the small street, rue Panonceaux, on which he lives in the Latin Quarter. Mr. Newell prefers to meet Garnett in the Luxembourg Gardens instead of at his small, inconspicuous apartment, which symbolizes his fall in financial stature. Rue Panonceaux is described as "a little melancholy back street, with lean old houses sweating rust and damp, and glimpses of pit-like gardens, black and sunless, between walls bristling with iron spikes . . . Garnett started to mount the ill-smelling stairs to the fourth floor, on which he learned from the concierge that Mr. Newell lodged." In this story Wharton uses the faubourg for setting and symbolism and gives a satiric though humorous portrait of Americans, at least in the person of Mrs. Newell, interested solely in the status that wealth can offer. (On a hopeful note, the young couple seem sincere in their affection for each other, although they are not very imaginative.)

*Invalides, avenue
des Champs-Elysées,
Luxembourg Gardens,
Opéra*

EXHIBITION OF PICTURES.

Works by Mlle Louise Abbema and M. René Foy in the Georges Petit Gallery.

VINCENT VAN GOGH'S PICTURES.

Show of the Societe Nouvelle de Peintres et Sculpteurs in the Rue de Seze.

An interesting exhibition of seventy-five pictures, studies and watercolors, by Mlle. Louise Abbema, who is a past-mistress in the art of painting flowers, has just been opened in the Petit Gallery.

All the gamut of the most varied species of flora has been exhausted to enable the artist to display her marvellous talent. Among the numerous compositions also exhibited by her I must mention some decorative designs for "salles de fête," and a sketch of a "Gismonda" for the crush-room of the Théâtre Sarah Bernhardt. These are interesting artistic efforts for a woman. This exhibition, which will remain open till the end of the month, is well worth a visit.

Artistic Jewels.

The same may be said of the collection of artistic jewels by M. René Foy, which are exhibited in the same gallery. This artist, whose work has been frequently mentioned in the HERALD, shows a fan, the leaves of which are covered with an allegorical composition by Mlle. Abbema, "La Naissance de la Perle." Each stick is a figurine of a woman, whose only adornment is a girdle of precious stones of different colors. The ends are decorated with mistletoe carved in ivory.

I should also mention a lorgnette handle, representing a girl enrolled in goat's beard; a silver waistband plate, with a head of a woman marvellously carved in ivory, and several pendants in exquisite taste, among them one decorated with designs inspired by pinks and set off with rose diamonds.

"Societe Nouvelle" Exhibition.

I was only able yesterday to visit the exhibition of the Société Nouvelle de Peintres et Sculpteurs in the rue de Sèze. If I speak of it at this late period, it is because I was greatly interested in some of the works, which will be on view until the 20th inst. M. René Prinet exhibits, among other things, three pictures which I consider remarkably fine. They are admirably drawn, especially the one entitled "Convalescence." They are at the same time vigorous, and yet quiet and severe in tone, especially a figure of a woman on a sofa beside the fire.

M. Gaston La Touche exhibits six most pleasing canvases. "L'Après-Midi," a composition singular, and extremely original, and "Le Dernier Chapitre," a picture with two half-length figures, are marvellously lighted up by rays coming through a curtain. A small canvas, "Le Bal," wherein the artist has succeeded in catching the movement and whirl of a ballroom in the midst of blazing warm light, is in every way remarkable

---

Ultra-Impressionism.

The small congregation of ultra-impressionists are in a state of great delight over the works of the late Vincent van Gogh, in the Bernheim Jeune exhibition, rue Laffitte. In spite of my sincere admiration for some of the painters of the young school, in spite of the place occupied by the works of some of the great impressionist landscape painters, in spite of my eclectic taste in matters of art, my delight in the exhibition of Van Gogh's works resolves itself into mild hilarity.

Portraits painted in globules, which look as if made with multi-colored wafers; sunflowers on a blue ground as a floral decoration; landscapes in which the palette knife has traced deep furrows in monochrome paste—these are the features over which very serious amateurs and erudite critics run wild. I am neither one nor the other; I can only laugh.

As to the artist, I gather from the correspondence introduced into the preface of the catalogue, that he was "intoxicated with colors." That is no doubt why he could not see straight. To delight in colors and to empty bladders of ultramarine, chrome or vermilion, on a malachite table does not suffice to render a man a painter.

I cannot seriously discuss any of the pictures that I saw, but I advise all those who like facetious things and caricatures to go to the Bernheim Jeune Gallery, rue Laffitte. They will not regret their visit.

An exhibition of the works of Trouillebert, recently deceased, will open to-day in the Galerie des Artistes Modernes, rue Caumartin.

THE SALON

Claude Monet's Works.

First of all I will mention Claude Monet, five of whose works figure in the catalogue, two of them in the first rank. No. 14, "Le Bassin d'Argenteuil," is an exquisite landscape, exquisitely delicate and full of luminous qualities. It measures 86cm. across by 60cm. high.

No. 17, "Vue de Sardam," by the same artist, is considered the gem of the sale. It is one of those views in Holland in which a canal is depicted, bordered with windmills and red-roofed houses, beneath a blue sky flecked with white clouds, reflected in its calm waters. The coloring is warm and golden, and time has given it an admirable patina. In spite of its great qualities I prefer the first-named picture to it. M. Strauss, the great picture collector, who bought Sisley's "Pont de Moret," at the Feydeau sale, admired it greatly yesterday, and will certainly not fail to watch over its destiny at the sale.

Daubigny, the famous landscape painter, who greatly admired Claude Monet, introduced him to M. Durand thirty years ago, bought a picture of him, and had it in his At the sale in 1878 considered worthy of bigny's works, and in a second sale of the Daubigny's studio. was the buyer. He do not expect it will to-morrow.

I do not care much for de la Creuse," nor for du Havre," but I great "Le Pont d'Argenteui trifle sad-looking, for it twilight, the reflections transparent, and the pic teresting.

Monet, who has succeeded in seizing and fixing effects of light, which had up to his time been regarded as beyond the reach of the artist's brush, revealed method of impression

---

transparent, and the picture is most in teresting.

Monet, who has succeeded in seizing and fixing effects of light, which had up to his time been regarded as beyond the reach of the artist's brush, revealed a new method of impression, and, as M. Thiébaud Sisson so justly says, has widened the limits of art.

Jongkind figures in the catalogue, but

SALES AT THE HOTEL DROUOT.

Important Impressionist Pictures by Monet, Sisley and Pissarro to Be Disposed Of To-morrow.

BEAUFRERE EFFECTS ON VIEW.

Many Drawings and Small Artistic Curios to Be Seen in Rooms 10 and 11 This Afternoon.

The collection of pictures formed by M. X——, which were on view privately yesterday, will be open to the public this afternoon in Room 6 at the Hotel Drouot. There are only thirty-eight works, but they indicate that the collector had a pronounced taste for the impressionist school, or, as M. Bernheim, the young expert in charge of the sale, well characterizes it, the school of 1870.

The names of Sisley, Claude Monet and Pissarro, in fact, occupy the chief place in the catalogue, and beneath them Guillaumin, Lebourg, Cottet, Gauguin and Vogler.

As is always the case on such occasions, there was a good deal of discussion yesterday on the merits of the collection as a whole, or of one or another isolated work. It would be out of place to sum up the various opinions that I heard, some based on personal interests, others on a manner of appreciation, due either to a too-advanced or too-incomplete education in art. I shall give my own opinion, which is extremely favorable to some of which will not fail to be made on it as a whole.

"Daunt Diana" is set in belle-époque Paris among American art collectors who frequented art sales at the Hotel Drouot and auctions at Christie's in London. "The Temperate Zone" concerns a shallow American couple spending the season at the Hotel Nouveau Luxe (a satirical name for the Ritz) in Paris. Their interest in art is focused on fads and the possible financial gains to be achieved by possessing desirable paintings. Their insensitivities are highlighted by their contrast to a genuine American connoisseur of art and literature.

In "In Trust," the goal of a wealthy young American is to introduce other youths to the aesthetic treasures of Europe so that they may escape the cultural barrenness of America. His plans involve "the ultimate aesthetic redemption of the whole human race, and provisionally restoring the sense of beauty to those unhappy millions of our fellow-countrymen who . . . now live and die in surroundings of unperceived and unmitigated ugliness."

Edith's novel *The Reef* (1912) is set in Paris and London. Traces of her own psychological development in her relationships with both Morton Fullerton and Walter Berry may be gleaned from the psychological development of *The Reef*'s characters, Anna Leath and Sophie Viner.

Wharton's writings also refer to her affair with Morton Fullerton. Her poem "Terminus" recounts a night they spent together at the Charing Cross Hotel, and her story "The Pretext" evokes their relationship. "The Letters," written in 1910, may represent an evaluation of the Fullerton affair. Set in Paris and its surrounding areas, it is the story of an American governess, Lizzie West, who will eventually marry Vincent Deering, the widowed father of her student. After his wife dies, Deering returns to New York. Lizzie writes him numerous love letters, which, she discovers after their marriage, he never read. The threads of Edith's life come together in this story. There are descriptions of the happiness of being near Paris. She describes the Parisian suburb of St. Cloud through the emotions of Lizzie West: "She noticed the first waves of wisteria over courtyard railings and the highlights of new foliage against the walls of ivy-matted gardens; and she thought again, as she had thought a hundred times before, that she had never seen so beautiful a spring." The invalid Mrs. Deering brings out Edith's resentment toward Teddy Wharton's increasingly disturbing illnesses; Mrs. Deering does not pay attention to her daughter, Juliet, continually rests upstairs "reading relays of dog-eared novels, the choice of which she left to the cook and the nurse," and is interested only in her novels and the " 'society notes' of the morning paper." Vincent Deering, a sort of dilettante American painter reminiscent of Fullerton, is nonetheless the man who first stirs Lizzie's passion. After their first kiss, "a sleeping germ of life thrilled and unfolded, and started out to seek the sun." He writes letters from the train and ship carrying him to America that are passionate commitments; Lizzie wavers between her desire to write and her fear of possible rejection. As she was "unused to the expression of personal emotion, she wavered between the impulse to pour out all she felt and the fear lest her extravagance should amuse or even bore him. She never lost the sense that what was to her the central crisis of experience must be a mere episode in a life so predestined as his to romantic incidents." This story, probably written shortly before the conclusion of the love affair between Edith and Morton Fullerton, provides the most compelling reasons for the affair and its end.

BEFORE AND DURING THE WAR

Book cover, The Reef,
first edition, 1912

Walter Berry returned to Paris from a diplomatic post in Cairo in July 1910 and was Edith Wharton's houseguest at 53, rue de Varenne while he searched for an apartment. He found one in rue Guillaume, very close to Wharton's home. Teddy Wharton's health was precarious, and he went to various spas and clinics both in America and in Europe. Fullerton, with whom Edith was on friendly terms, became a freelance journalist. She visited Berenson at the Villa I Tatti in the hills surrounding Florence in the fall of 1911 and Henry James in London in December. The Mount was sold in January 1912 and during that year she traveled in France, England, and Italy. By this time, the Whartons' marriage was no longer viable and they were divorced in Paris in April 1913.

Wharton's first intimation of the devastation of World War I occurred on a June afternoon in 1914 when she was visiting Jacques-Emile Blanche in Auteuil, a suburb of Paris. In her memoir she contrasts the beautiful day with talk of the arts and the news of the assassination at Sarajevo:

> It was a perfect summer day; brightly dressed groups were gathered at tea-tables beneath the overhanging boughs, or walking up and down the flower-bordered turf. Broad bands of blue forget-me-nots edged the shrubberies, old-fashioned *corbeilles* of yellow and bronze wall-flowers dotted the lawn, the climbing roses were budding on the pillars of the porch . . . An exceptionally gay season was drawing to its close, the air was full of new literary and artistic emotions, and that dust of ideas with which the atmosphere of Paris is always laden sparkled like motes in the sun. I joined a party at one of the tables, and as we sat there a cloud-shadow swept over us, abruptly darkening bright flowers and bright dresses. "Haven't you heard? The Archduke Ferdinand assassinated . . . at Sarajevo . . . Where *is* Sarajevo? His wife was with him. What was her name? Both shot dead."

By August France and Germany were at war. Americans and other foreigners in France at the time had problems securing funds, as assets were

THE REEF

EDITH WHARTON

frozen at the war's outbreak. Through the help of Walter Berry, Edith quickly overcame this obstacle and put her considerable energy, connections, and resources at the service of the war effort.

She opened a workroom for unemployed seamstresses on rue de l'Université and secured orders for their work among her numerous connections in the United States and in France. She was the director of the American Hostels for Refugees and used her sensitivity to the homeless and her keen organizing ability, along with the use of several buildings belonging to wealthy acquaintances, to set up free or nominal-charge housing for the refugees. R. W. B. Lewis summarizes her housing aid in *Edith Wharton:*

> The building in the Rue Brochant supplied free furnished rooms for families with seven or more children and for husbandless women with children; the place on the Avenue Félix-Faure rented housing to some two hundred refugees at the equivalent of $1.50 a month per room, with light, heat, and washing included; the large apartment house in the Rue de la Quintinie took in as many more. In the Rue Taitbout, meals were distributed at nominal prices to nearly six hundred persons a day.

Wharton also established a free medical clinic, a clothing center, a discount food center, a nursery that offered classes in singing, sewing, and English, and an employment agency. She ably administered all of these enterprises in various parts of Paris by forming and supervising nine committees of volunteers.

In 1915 Edith and Walter Berry went to the front in Argonne and brought supplies to the medical units. Wharton visited various fronts several times in 1915 and reported on her visits in articles that were published in *Scribner's* magazine or in New York newspapers. These articles were collected in the volume *Fighting France from Dunkerque to Belfort* (1915). Also in 1915, Edith edited *The Book of the Homeless,* a compilation of literature, prose, music, and art by accomplished creative artists, whom Wharton persuaded to donate their work to benefit her refugee relief projects. In 1916 she started work on programs to aid French soldiers and civilians afflicted with tuberculosis. For her work with French and Belgian refugees, she was made a Chevalier of the Legion of Honor in April 1916, and in 1918 she received the Medal of Queen Elizabeth from King Albert of Belgium.

LITERARY ACTIVITY IN THE WAR YEARS

Despite her tremendous expenditure of time and effort in relief work, Wharton also published fiction during this period. Her novella *Summer* (1917) is a companion volume to *Ethan Frome* and concerns the coming of age of a poor young woman in the isolated landscape of the Berkshire region in Massachusetts. Interestingly, the character Lucius Harney is a young architect who is studying eighteenth-century houses in rural New England. His interest is passed on to the heroine, Charity, when: "She noticed the fan-shaped tracery of the broken light above the door, the flutings of the paintless pilasters at the corners, and the round window set in the gable." *Summer*'s young lovers visit these older homes, which symbolize their ageless story of courtship. Wharton's poem "Within the Tide" (1919) is a eulogy for her friend and distant relative Theodore Roosevelt. Her novel *The Marne* (1918) demonstrates her sensitivity to the catastrophic impact of the Great War.

A collection, *Xingu and Other Stories,* was published in 1916, featuring several tales on French themes. "Coming Home" is set in World War I France during the German occupation. "Autres Temps" and "The Long Run" were written before the war. "Autres Temps" concerns the social stigma a divorced woman who has been living abroad faces when she returns to visit Old New York society and her ensuing feelings of loneliness. This may reflect the painful Wharton divorce. "The Long Run" chronicles the choice a privileged man has made not to forge a permanent bond with the woman he loves, although she appears willing to endure the social ostracism a break with her past will cause. Both of these tales describe the price that is paid by completely conforming to or completely ignoring society and its constraints. These were issues Wharton was grappling with in the prewar and possibly in the war years, as they are recurrent themes in her later fiction. Her divorce and her decision to live in France demonstrate a certain isolation from her native American society. Of course, the difficulties of the war period overshadowed some of these concerns. As a respite from some of her cares, she took a trip to Morocco with Walter Berry in 1917. At about this time, Edith formed an affectionate friendship with a young American, Ronald Simmons, who was studying art history in Paris. When the United States entered the war, he enlisted in Paris and soon after succumbed to pneumonia. Edith dedicated her novel *The Marne* to him, as well as *A Son at the Front,* which was published in 1923.

After the horrors of wartime all of Paris rejoiced on Armistice Day in November 1918. In *A Backward Glance* Edith describes hearing the joyful news:

> The quarter I lived in was so quiet in those days that, except for the crash of aerial battles, few sounds disturbed it; but now I was startled to hear, at an unusual hour, the familiar bell of our nearest church, Sainte Clothilde. I went to the balcony and all the household followed me. Through the deep expectant hush we heard, one after another, the bells of Paris calling to each other.

Illustration (by Walter Gay), The Book of the Homeless, *1915*

The Ile-de-France
and the Riviera
1919–1937

DURING THE LAST YEARS OF THE WAR, EDITH WHARTON BEGAN TO SEARCH FOR a home outside Paris. Her exhausting relief work and her emotional distress due to the desperate conditions at the front, coupled with the noise and crowds of Paris during the 1919 peace conference, made her seek more appealing surroundings. It became imperative for her to find a home in the French countryside.

ST. BRICE-SOUS-FORET

A small estate, Jean-Marie, on the Ile-de-France, about twelve miles north of Paris, came on the market. The estate was large enough to provide a pastoral setting; Edith had room to arrange several garden areas with flowering fruit trees. She restored the estate's original name, Pavillon Colombe, perhaps out of interest in its history. (Two Venetian sisters, actresses with the Comédie Italienne, both adopted the stage name Colombe. They lived at the estate in the eighteenth century due to the largesse of their lovers, one an English lord.)

The Pavillon Colombe, with its colorful history, was to be Edith's summer and autumn home for the rest of her life. She would spend the winter and spring months at a rented villa, Le Bocage during the winter of 1920 and Ste. Claire du Vieux Château thereafter (which she later purchased), both on the Riviera at Hyères. Her furniture from the rue de Varenne apartment followed her to the Pavillon Colombe and Ste. Claire.

At both residences, Edith engaged in one of her most satisfying pur-

PAVILLON COLOMBE

Main door on the rue de Paris

PAVILLON COLOMBE

Iron grillwork door to the grounds and garden facade, probably in the 1920s

suits—creating pleasurable homes and gardens. In her memoir she recalls the thrill of finding the Pavillon Colombe and its tranquil, restorative atmosphere:

> The way there . . . was through pleasant market-gardens, and acres of pear and apple orchard. The orchards were just bursting into bloom, and we seemed to pass through a rosy snow-storm to reach what was soon to be my own door. I saw the house, and fell in love with it in spite of its dirt and squalour—and before the end of the war it was mine. At last I was to have a garden again—and a big old kitchen-garden as well, planted with ancient pear and apple trees espaliered and in cordon, and an old pool full of fat old gold-fish; and silence and rest under big trees!

In August 1919, Edith opened her home to her friends for a celebration. Guests included Bernard Berenson, Abbé Mugnier, the Walter Gays, Charles du Bos, John Hugh Smith, the Paul Bourgets, Gaillard Lapsley, and Percy Lubbock. Her move to the Pavillon had once more established her in a supportive and sympathetic circle, and she could devote herself to its furnishings and gardens.

PAVILLON COLOMBE EXTERIORS

The Pavillon Colombe is in the northern suburbs of Paris in the French *département*, or region, known as Seine-et-Oise—the juncture of the Seine and Oise Rivers. Tall doors on the village street, rue de Paris, permit entry into the home. The view of the street (north) facade is not indicative of the tranquil beauty of the villa itself or of the gardens, orchards, and lawns fanning out from its south facade. There is a decorative iron grillwork door at the entrance to the grounds of the villa; a path leads to the south and west facades. The south facade has three sets of French doors in its central section; above each is a round window set partway into the roof. One side has four windows, those above being slightly smaller, and the other has French doors on the ground level with windows above. Both the doors and windows were shuttered, although they are not at the present time. One section of the villa, which includes three sets of French doors under dormer windows, runs into the east side of the south facade at a right angle. These French doors were

PAVILLON COLOMBE

*Views of the south
facade, probably in the
1920s; exterior view*

PAVILLON COLOMBE

Drawing room (above and opposite) and dining room, probably in the 1920s

not original, as earlier photographs show them to be rectangular glass doors covered by bamboo shades, suggesting that the interior was a sunroom. The later French doors open onto the expanse of the gravel path and garden.

PAVILLON COLOMBE INTERIORS

The ground floor of the Pavillon Colombe is similar to that of The Mount. R. W. B. Lewis summarizes the basic plan in *Edith Wharton:*

> The six rooms on the ground floor, from the library to the dining room, opened one into the other, and each opened onto the narrow walk running along the south side. It was almost exactly like The Mount, though the order of the rooms was reversed, and it revealed again Edith Wharton's basic principle in the arrangement of house interiors. Each room was distinctly itself, one never had

the impression (as Edith remembered having in her parents' New York home) of being half in one room and half in another; yet the several rooms flowed together to create an atmosphere of unity and quiet harmony.

These rooms were furnished with a combination of pieces Edith had transferred from her rue de Varenne apartment and, most probably, other pieces she had and newly purchased ones, both antiques and reproductions.

The dining room was the furthest on the west and featured wood-paneled walls topped by a simple cornice. The floor is marble with a diamond pattern, and two marble tables were set into the walls. The larger marble console featured Louis XVI figures and a neoclassical wreath as its base. The room was lighted with wall sconces. The dining furniture consisted of painted-wood Louis XVI–style chairs with cane backs and a painted-wood table. A bust in the classical style topped a pedestal in a niche in a wall

panel. A marble lavabo, which may have had water issuing from a marble ornament in its basin, stood in a similar wall niche. The two available photographs reveal different removable carpets, one of which appears to be Chinese. The Chinese motif was also present in a vase in front of the mirror on the larger marble console and a smaller Chinese vase on the marble corner console.

The dining room opened to the good-sized drawing room, which Edith graced with Italianate mirrors, wall sconces, and eighteenth-century furniture, including Louis XV chairs and settees, an elegantly decorated Louis XVI commode with a Chinese figure and stand, Louis XVI stands bearing Chinese vases, a small Louis XVI table holding what appears to be a dried floral arrangement, and a small French worktable, or *tricoteuse,* holding a statue of a bird. A decorative clock stood on the fireplace mantel below a mirrored overmantel. There was an interesting Chinese stand in front of the fireplace. The hardwood floor was covered by small carpets. Small-scale prints and paintings were tastefully displayed against light-colored walls.

The drawing room led to a sitting room that featured a Louis XVI chimney piece and a Louis XVI bergère with curved ottoman beside a round reading table whose base was decorated by a delicate female figure. In front of a decorative Chinese screen stood a small-scale Louis XVI chair. The walls featured Chinese decorative paper and wall sconces. Small carpets were placed on the dark hardwood floor. Other objets d'art included Chinese porcelain vases, a Louis XVI ormolu clock, and biscuit de Sèvres cherubs.

The sitting room opened onto a very small boudoir that at one time held a canopied bed. Plaster doves hung over the bed at the center of the archway as a reminder of the villa's former inhabitants, the Colombe sisters. The room's carpet was Middle Eastern. The barely visible carpet point under the small boudoir chair was to be placed toward Mecca. The juxtaposition of the plasterwork doves and the prayer rug lent a certain humorous irony to the room.

The boudoir led to another small room and then into the library, which featured a Louis XVI *bureau plat* desk and elegant caned Regency chair. Edith's inkwell, executed in white faience, was of the Empire period. Library furnishings included built-in bookcases, Louis XVI paneling and chimney piece, Louis XV fauteuils and settee, a smaller Louis XV chair in front of a Louis XV decorative screen, and a Louis XIV stool near the library table. Two matching small tables may have been Chinese lacquerwork. Other elegant decorative objects included a Louis XVI ormolu clock and figures, probably Chinese, and a Chinese porcelain vase on the mantle. Behind the library was a bathroom, which had a wooden bathtub and brass faucets in the shape of swans' heads.

Pavillon Colombe

Sitting room and library, probably in the 1920s; Edith Wharton at her writing desk ca. 1925

PAVILLON COLOMBE

Garden furniture and statuary (during Wharton's ownership)

PAVILLON COLOMBE GARDENS

Guests at the Pavillon Colombe enjoyed elegant and tasteful surroundings in the interior of the villa and were also able to enjoy the various garden areas, which were arranged in Edith Wharton's time as garden "rooms." Unfortunately not many photographs of the garden from her time survive, but those that do portray the various outdoor "rooms." The French doors on the ground floor of the villa offered views and access to the garden spaces. Lawn furniture was often arranged on or close to the gravel path.

The gardens followed the principles of *Italian Villas and Their Gardens* in their use of the three chief elements of garden design: marble, water, and "perennial verdure." Flowers also had a significant position in the Pavillon gardens. Classical busts on pedestals peeped out from foliage-covered niches, stone urns overflowed with flowers, and cherubs with baskets of flowers adorned garden paths.

A formal lawn area with trimmed circular hedges currently graces the exterior of the south facade. During Edith's residence it appears that this area featured well-groomed shrubs and fruit trees. Other areas, at various times either manicured lawns or wooded clearings, were enhanced by statuary.

PAVILLON COLOMBE

Gardens with statuary

PAVILLON COLOMBE

Views of statuary

PAVILLON COLOMBE

Flower-filled urns and glade with statue, probably in the 1920s

Each garden area had a unique atmosphere. A stone well with decorative ironwork stood before a garden trellis in one location. The gardens also featured stone paths with flower borders. A tranquil hedge-bordered garden path was shaded by a wooden lattice of foliage. An often-photographed garden area was the fountain pool, with its statue of Pan holding a stream of water. Benches recessed into the hedges provided a solitary respite for the garden stroller. A watercolor of the area was done by Edith's friend Robert Norton.

Edith's rose garden surrounded an oval water-lily-laden pond. In 1925 she wrote to her friend Daisy (Margaret Terry) Chanler about her plans for this garden: "I got your splendid tulip-list, for which all gratitude, & am ordering from Van Tubergen. My new rose-garden is promising, & I find this soil so decidedly made for rose growing that I mean to plant hundreds more this autumn, & to root up nearly all the old varieties. The new ones are so much more worth while, & one can now get varieties of every kind to which mildew is unknown."

Edith's plans for writing in tranquillity and gardening were realized at the Pavillon Colombe. She was treated to frequent visits from her close circle of friends and found her life there quite satisfying. The Pavillon Colombe is currently one of the residences of Prince Philipp and Princess Isabelle von Liechtenstein.

PAVILLON COLOMBE

Arbor, fountain pool

Pavillon Colombe

*Procession for the Feast
of the Assumption
around the fountain
pool in 1936, views of
the oval pond (during
Wharton's ownership)*

PAVILLON COLOMBE

Watercolor (by Robert Norton) of the fountain pool; stone path with flower border, probably in the 1920s

THE RIVIERA

Edith wished to escape the feverish crowds of Paris during the 1919 peace conference, and as repairs were still underway at the Pavillon Colombe, she decided to plan a stay of several months on the Riviera. She was accompanied by Robert Norton, a former member of the British Admiralty and an accomplished watercolorist. The two had complementary personalities and developed a friendship during their sojourn in Hyères, a little-known part of the Riviera, which provided a soothing climate and refreshing atmosphere that Edith found especially restorative. Soon she was hoping to purchase a property in this location to serve as her winter residence. She found a former convent that had been constructed within the fortified walls of a castle, possibly built as early as the twelfth century. Sisters of Saint Claire, *les Clarisses,* had resided there, and the villa received the formal name Ste. Claire du Vieux Château. Extensive repairs and refurbishing were required at the villa but Edith was determined to see her plan through. The villa was rented on a long lease and she established her household there in December 1920; she purchased the estate in 1927. Life in her Riviera surroundings followed the same pattern as that of the summer and fall at the Pavillon Colombe. Wharton worked in the early morning hours, had a quiet lunch or picnicked with her guests, enjoyed visiting the surrounding area or took an afternoon stroll. She made her second large-scale home in France suitable to her various requirements.

STE. CLAIRE EXTERIORS

The site of Ste. Claire is one of its most appealing attributes. R. W. B. Lewis describes it succinctly in *Edith Wharton:* "The location was splendid, with a view down over the rooftops of Hyères to the Mediterranean and the thin strip of land that curved out to the wooded rise of the Giens peninsula; to the left and right, like blurred dots in the distance, were the Isles of Gold; farther away still loomed the Maritime Alps." Its hillside setting provided many long-distance vistas as well as a view of the tower of a nearby Romanesque church. Edith herself describes her pleasure at moving into Ste. Claire shortly before Christmas 1920 in a letter to her sister-in-law Mary Cadwalader Jones:

> Yesterday was the happiest Xmas I have spent in many a long year. I can wish no old woman of my age a better one! The little house is delicious, so friendly & comfortable, & full of sun & air; but what overwhelms us all—though we

*Aerial view of an island
near Hyères*

STE. CLAIRE

Watercolor (by Robert Norton), views of the tower and facade in the 1920s–1930s

thought we knew it—is the endless beauty of the view, or rather the views, for we look south, east & west, "miles & miles," & our quiet-coloured end of evening presents us with a full moon standing over the tower of the great romanesque church just below the house, & a sunset silhouetting the "Iles d'Or" in black on a sea of silver . . . Yesterday we had the divinest Riviera weather, & as we sat on the terrace in the sun taking our coffee after luncheon a joint groan of deliverance escaped us at the thought of London, New York & Paris.

STE. CLAIRE INTERIORS

The ground floor of Ste. Claire was arranged in a fashion somewhat similar to those of The Mount and the Pavillon Colombe, and the rooms themselves closely follow the principles of design in *The Decoration of Houses*. The hallway had a marble floor in a diamond pattern and a light-colored plain dado. The upper walls were covered in paper, or possibly fabric, in a Chinese pattern. Wall coverings are not generally recommended in *The Decoration of*

STE. CLAIRE

Facade and courtyard in the 1920s–1930s, watercolor (by Robert Norton)

STE. CLAIRE

Hallway and dining room in the 1920s–1930s

Houses, but the treatment does blend harmoniously with the Chinese painted-glass lantern that illuminated the room. Two cabinets with decorated front panels were set into the corners at each side of French doors. The furniture consisted of a simple wood table and chairs with elegantly designed backs. A decorative clock and mirror adorned the walls as did vases of fresh flowers, an important decorative touch in most of the rooms at Ste. Claire during Wharton's residence.

The dining room featured light-painted wood-paneled walls and the same type of marble flooring as the hall, partially covered by a removable carpet. The ceiling cornice was understated and the lighting was provided by wall sconces. The white-painted wood table and chairs gave the room a light feeling. The Louis XVI dining chairs surrounded a table that was probably of later vintage. A dark hardwood console holding decorative candle lamps and smaller serving tables of similar wood completed the furnishings. A decorative screen, possibly Chinese, provided added visual interest.

The furnishings of the drawing room had the same tasteful elegance as the hall and dining room. Photographs that appear to have been taken at two different periods show that at one stage a paper or possibly fabric wall treatment was added, a Louis XV settee had muslin-covered and then upholstered loose pillows, and a large patterned carpet took the place of small ones. Both sets of photographs show a Louis XV chimney piece that included a three-part mirror and medallion painting of a man and woman in court attire. Mantel ornaments included twin figures of Atlas. Other furnishings at various times included Louis XV and Louis XVI chairs, a chaise, and an Empire table and *bonheur du jour* cabinet flanking the door. Other elements were hardwood bookcases and ample tables, generally topped with books and seasonal flower arrangements. Edith's garden flowers found a home among the several paintings of floral arrangements in the drawing room as well as among the various small-scale statues and decorative vases.

The rather roomy drawing room was complemented by a smaller sitting/reading room, which had a marble fireplace with mirrored overmantel framed by a lattice design and crowned with an urn and flowing garlands. Cozy upholstered chairs, ample lighting, an inviting bookcase, and a library table completed Wharton's furnishings. Two windows along perpendicular walls featured valenced curtains, a treatment not generally recommended by Edith, but it may be that the opening in the corner of the room was actually a door and the treatment used formed a portiere rather than an actual window curtain. Edith did not generally favor portieres, either, but in this case may have used the treatments for symmetry. Three arched windows in the room provided a view of the gardens; cut flowers in dainty vases brought the extensive gardens inside.

STE. CLAIRE

Views of the morning room in the 1920s–1930s

STE. CLAIRE

Views of the drawing room in the 1920s–1930s

STE. CLAIRE

Views of the reading room in the 1920s–1930s

To provide herself and her guests with ample reading material, Edith created a new library for Ste. Claire with a brown brick floor partially covered by small rugs. It featured numerous light-colored wood bookcases set into the walls and also jutting into the room to provide for Edith's wide-ranging collection of volumes, some of fine craftsmanship. The bookcases jutting into the library may have been placed between the windows on one side. Long library tables, reading tables, comfortable chairs, lamps, and smaller tables gave the library an inviting yet serious air. In addition to the library, four ample guest rooms on the second floor also resulted from the massive remodeling project.

STE. CLAIRE

Edith Wharton and her housekeeper, Catharine Gross, on the terrace ca. 1920–1930

STE. CLAIRE GARDENS

Since there were spectacular views on three sides of the villa, the terrace and gardens were favorite gathering and resting spots for Wharton and her guests. Edith was often photographed on the terrace enjoying her surroundings and resting on sturdy wicker furniture with festive striped cushions or hardy wooden garden benches and chairs. Robert Norton painted several atmospheric watercolors of the exterior of the villa, one featuring a view of a portion of the terrace with flowers in bloom.

Edith noted her plant choices for a garden in a letter to Mary Cadwalader Jones. Unfortunately, she was cataloguing the losses her gardens sustained during a severe frost in December 1920. She wrote:

> My terraces were just beginning to be full of bursting sprouting things, & it was really sickening to see the black crepy rags which, a few hours before, were heliotropes, "anthemises," tradescantia, plumbago, arums, geraniums—all the stock-in-trade of a Riviera garden—dangling woefully from the denuded terraces.

STE. CLAIRE

*Watercolor (by Robert
Norton); Edith
Wharton standing
at the entrance to the
courtyard, probably
in the 1930s*

STE. CLAIRE

*Edith Wharton on the
terrace ca. 1920–1930*

STE. CLAIRE

*Terrace in the
1920s–1930s*

The orange trees were severely frozen, & some of the old ones may be lost; & even my splendid old caroube trees, which had put on their glorious dense shining foliage in October, are all frizzled & brown. Eucalyptus & pepper-trees are shrivelled up, & the huge prickly pears that were the pride of the place are falling apart like paper flowers the day after a procession. Even the native wildflowers, acanthus, fennel and valerian, hung limp from their roots, & are only just picking up . . . I had a magnificent climbing buddleya which covered one of my highest terrace walls, and was just preparing to hang out its hundreds of yellow plumes—it is as bare as a ship's rigging in a gale!

Besides these plants and trees, historic photographs show that the garden had lawn areas with flower and shrub borders, rustic garden seats, and arched topiary. Edith was always very affected by the fate of her gardens, and when gale winds and unusually low temperatures destroyed her Ste. Claire gardens again in January and February of 1929, she was devastated. Shortly thereafter she developed a serious illness, but she recovered and continued to write, travel, and garden.

TRAVELS AND LITERARY ACTIVITY

Between 1919 and her death in 1937, Edith enjoyed and satisfied her yearning for travel. She spent several weeks a year in England visiting friends and keeping up with their latest intellectual forays. She received an honorary doctorate from Yale University and traveled to America for the last time to

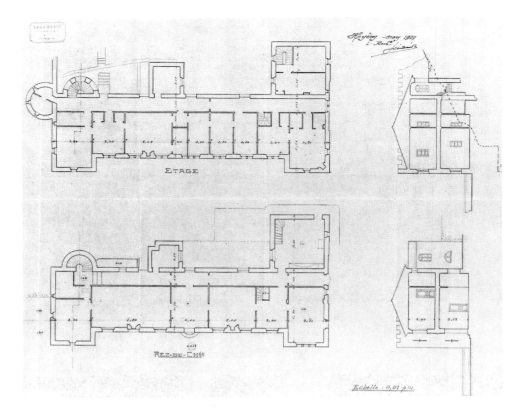

STE. CLAIRE

*Plans and sections (drawn
by Léon David, 1909)*

receive it. Always fascinated with classical literature and art, she rented a yacht, the *Osprey,* and with several friends embarked on a ten-week cruise through the Aegean, visiting many of the same sites she and Teddy had seen on their first Aegean cruise and exploring several that had been inaccessible, including Delphi, Mistra, Cyprus, and Crete. Edith reports in *A Backward Glance* that she was always restored by traveling: "I am born happy every morning, and during that magical cruise nothing ever seemed to occur during the day to diminish my beatitude . . . These and other wanderings have been the highlights of the last years; when I turn from them the sky darkens." Her writing may have also provided some light and comfort in her last years, and she continued her literary pursuits as well.

Wharton's literary output during the time roughly corresponding to her life at St. Brice and Hyères reflected her new life in France and her memories and understanding of the life of her childhood and even that of her ancestors in Old New York, as well as musings on the craft of writing. The Pulitzer Prize–winning *Age of Innocence* depicts 1870s Old New York society clearly and at times scathingly. Entrapment in the rules and rituals of the "tribe" leads to a lack of emotional fulfillment, yet separation from these rules leads to loneliness and isolation. More than a novel of manners, *The Age of Innocence* describes how outward style affects psychological substance.

In her series *Old New York* (1924), she describes the world of her parents and grandparents in four novellas covering the four decades between 1840 and 1880. In *False Dawn,* a young gentleman of Old New York makes the grand tour of Europe before his marriage and selects masterworks of paintings for his father's collection. Yet his father has heard of none of them, and the young man is disinherited, receiving at his father's death only the paintings. He believes in them and keeps them, but it is not until after his death that their true value is known. *The Old Maid* tells the story of a young woman in Old New York who has an illegitimate child. Since she cannot openly care for her daughter, she engages in work with orphans so that she can be near the little girl. She is unable to marry, for she cannot tell a husband about the child, but her cousin arranges to raise the child as her own. Her anguish at being separated from her daughter pervades her entire life. In *The Spark* a middle-aged wife engages in numerous extramarital affairs; her husband finally reacts to one of her suitors, but in the interest of keeping the peace and not making a scene, the truth goes untold and the couple remains married. While suffering from a wound during the Civil War, the husband meets Walt Whitman and is influenced by Whitman's generous personality but does not recognize the genius of his poetry. The final novella, *New Year's Day,* is set in the same period as *The Age of Innocence,* the 1870s, and fea-

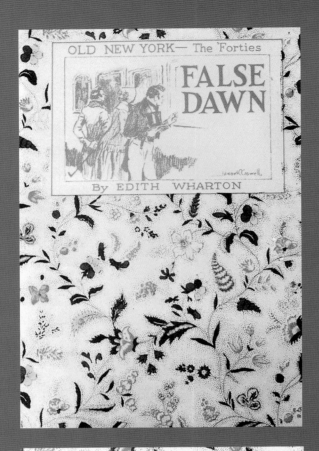

OLD NEW YORK — The 'Forties

FALSE DAWN

By EDITH WHARTON

OLD NEW YORK — The 'Fifties

THE OLD MAID

By EDITH WHARTON

OLD NEW YORK — The 'Sixties

THE SPARK

By EDITH WHARTON

OLD NEW YORK — The 'Seventies

NEW YEAR'S DAY

By EDITH WHARTON

THE
GLIMPSES
of the MOON
EDITH WHARTON

Book covers (opposite),
Old New York *series,
first editions, 1924
(artwork by Edward C.
Caswell); book jacket,*
The Glimpses of the
Moon, *first edition,
1922*

tures some of the same characters. An adulterous woman finds that after the death of her relatively young husband, she cannot become involved with anything other than her betrayal of him and her remorse. These four novellas have an acute sense of place—the stifling drawing rooms and suffocating decor are aptly and poignantly drawn—and sense of time. The freshness of art and poetry further underscores the airless nature of elaborate drawing rooms filled with unimaginative inhabitants.

In the novel *The Mother's Recompense* (1925), a mother, who has left her stultifying husband and young daughter in Old New York, returns after World War I to find her daughter engaged to her former lover. She is unable to fit back into the "tribe" and eventually returns to her life in Europe. *The Glimpses of the Moon* (1922) was set in the 1920s and is not as searching as the tales featuring Old New York but does have evocative scenes set in Venice, Paris, Fontainebleau, and the Italian lake district. *Twilight Sleep* (1927) describes its young heroine, and by implication young women from proper families, as living in a blinded condition, hampered by the restrictions placed on them by society.

The Children (1928) concerns a band of youngsters headed by their eldest sister; they are in danger of separation and dislocation due to the marital whims of their various parents and stepparents. Not as badly off as World War I orphans, the children are still the victims of irresponsible adults, who while they care for their young financially, do not take into account their emotional and intellectual needs. It is an unusual novel in that it is a tale about children, both girls and boys, written for an adult audience. Its main characters are seven youths, all convincingly drawn, a feat with few parallels in American literature.

The companion novels *Hudson River Bracketed* (1929) and *The Gods Arrive* (1932) concern the coming of age and artistic struggles of a young American writer who must try to reconcile the pursuit of literature with his national and personal identity. He is very interested in the architecture and inhabitants of a Hudson River Valley home called the Willows, loosely based on Wyndcliffe, the home of Edith's aunt. The Willows was built in 1830 and was an example of the Hudson River Bracketed style of architecture. *The Buccaneers*, published posthumously in 1938, is the story of young American women on a crusade to marry British royalty.

Wharton's short stories were collected in four volumes: *Here and*

STE. CLAIRE

Edith Wharton on the terrace ca. 1920–1930

Beyond (1926), *Certain People* (1930), *The World Over* (1936), and *Ghosts* (1936). They include "Roman Fever," a witty, dramatic tale about two older women in which the more self-possessed discovers that her husband is the father of her companion's child. "After Holbein" concerns an elderly New York hostess, possibly based on Mrs. Astor, who has delusions that she is still receiving guests. "The Day of the Funeral" details the results of marital infidelity and cruelty.

Edith's nonfiction also took several interesting directions at this time. She described her observations of French culture in *French Ways and Their Meaning* (1919). She was impressed by the role of French women in intellectual conversations at salons. Although they mostly listened and did not talk, they were privy to conversation about ideas and their presence was taken for granted. *In Morocco* (1920) detailed her adventurous trip. In *The Writing of Fiction* (1925) she reflects on the craft by referring to such major writers as Balzac, Jane Austen, George Eliot, Stendhal, Trollope, Thackeray, Tolstoy, and Dostoyevsky. Her memoir, *A Backward Glance,* was published in 1934.

LAST GIFTS

On a voyage to the Pavillon Colombe from Ste. Claire in late May 1937, Wharton stopped at the Château de Grégy, Ogden Codman Jr.'s home. While there she suffered a stroke. In early June she was taken to the Pavillon Colombe. She was comfortable there and was sometimes able to enjoy the garden. She died on August 11.

Edith precisely recorded how she wished to distribute her property and possessions. The war committee known as the Committee of American Convalescent Homes was to be revived under the supervision of Elisina Royall Tyler. Edith wished to have her property used as a hospice for those inflicted with incurable tuberculosis and a treatment center for those with curable tuberculosis. Although her property was eventually privately bequeathed, her wishes, made known in a 1928 letter, show her sensitivity to the respite a suitable restorative place can provide the sick.

Edith had purchased a plot for herself near the grave of her beloved friend Walter Berry at the Cimetière des Gonards. An honor guard composed of old and new friends and war veterans gathered in the courtyard of the Pavillon Colombe for her funeral procession. At the Versailles cemetery another honor guard of veterans marched with the procession to the grave. The cemetery in Versailles, despite its proximity to the château, is modest and tranquil, a suitable resting place for Edith Wharton.

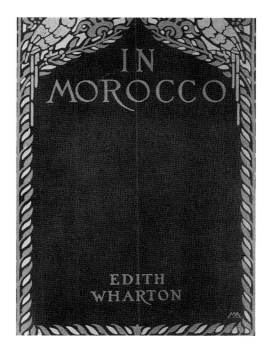

Book cover,
In Morocco,
first edition, 1920

Cimetière des Gonards,
Versailles: general view,
Edith Wharton's tombstone

Selected Bibliography and Information Sources

WORKS BY EDITH WHARTON

These works are arranged in order of original publication. Many are available in reprint editions and in selected collections by various publishers. Names of individual short stories are not included.

Verses (1878)
The Decoration of Houses (with Ogden Codman Jr.; 1897)
The Greater Inclination (1899)
The Touchstone (1900)
Crucial Instances (1901)
The Valley of Decision (two volumes; 1902)
The Descent of Man and Other Stories (1904)
Italian Villas and Their Gardens (1904)
Italian Backgrounds (1905)
The House of Mirth (1905)
Madame de Treymes (1907)
The Fruit of the Tree (1907)
The Hermit and the Wild Woman and Other Stories (1908)
A Motor-Flight Through France (1908)
Artemis to Actaeon and Other Verses (1909)
Tales of Men and Ghosts (1910)
Ethan Frome (1911)
The Reef (1912)
The Custom of the Country (1913)
Fighting France from Dunkerque to Belfort (1915)
Xingu and Other Stories (1916)
Summer (1917)
The Marne (1918)
French Ways and Their Meaning (1919)
In Morocco (1920)
The Age of Innocence (1920)
The Glimpses of the Moon (1922)
A Son at the Front (1923)
Old New York (four volumes; 1924)
The Mother's Recompense (1925)
The Writing of Fiction (1925)
Twelve Poems (1926)
Here and Beyond (1926)
Twilight Sleep (1927)
The Children (1928)
Hudson River Bracketed (1929)
Certain People (1930)
The Gods Arrive (1932)
Human Nature (1933)
A Backward Glance (1934)
The World Over (1936)
Ghosts (1937)
The Buccaneers (1938)
Fast and Loose: A Novelette (by David Olivieri [pseudonym]; edited by Viola Hopkins Winner; 1977)
The Letters of Edith Wharton (edited by R. W. B. Lewis and Nancy Lewis; 1988)

Auchincloss, Louis. *Edith Wharton: A Woman in Her Time*. New York: Harper & Row, 1975.

Bayley, John Barrington. "The Decoration of Houses as a Practical Handbook." Introductory essay, *The Decoration of Houses*. Reprint, New York: W. W. Norton, 1978.

Coles, William A. "The Genesis of a Classic." Introductory essay, *The Decoration of Houses*. Reprint, New York: W. W. Norton, 1978.

Dorsey, Hebe. *The Belle Epoque in the Paris Herald*. London: Thames and Hudson, 1986.

Fryer, Judith. *Felicitous Space: The Imaginative Structures of Edith Wharton and Willa Cather*. Chapel Hill: University of North Carolina Press, 1986.

Grafton, John. *New York in the Nineteenth Century*. 2nd ed. New York: Dover Publications, 1980.

Gannon, Thomas. *Newport Mansions*. Introduction by David Chase. Photography by Richard Cheek. Compton, R.I.: Fort Church Publishers, 1982.

Hayes, Thomas S. "Edith Wharton's Italian Gardens at The Mount." Introductory essay, *Italian Villas and Their Gardens*. Reprint, New York: W. W. Norton, 1988.

Joslin, Katherine. *Edith Wharton*. London: Macmillan, 1991.

Lewis, R. W. B. *Edith Wharton: A Biography*. New York: Harper & Row, 1975. Reprint, New York: Fromm International Publishing, 1985.

Lowe, David Garrard. *Stanford White's New York*. New York: Doubleday, 1992.

Lucie-Smith, Edward. *Furniture*. London: Thames and Hudson, 1979.

Marshall, Scott. *The Mount: A Historic Structure Report*. Albany: Mount Ida Press, 1996.

Reed, Henry Hope. "Edith Wharton and the Classical Landscape in America." Essay, *Italian Villas and Their Gardens*. Reprint, New York: W. W. Norton, 1988.

Ross, Arthur. Foreword, *Italian Villas and Their Gardens*. Reprint, New York: W. W. Norton, 1988.

Schriber, Mary Suzanne. Introduction, *A Motor-Flight Through France*. Reprint, DeKalb: Northern Illinois University Press, 1991.

Stasz, Clarice. *The Vanderbilt Women*. New York: St. Martin's Press, 1991.

Wilson, Richard Guy. "Edith and Ogden: Writing, Decoration, and Architecture." In *Ogden Codman and the Decoration of Houses*. Edited by Pauline C. Metcalf. Boston: David Godine, 1989.

Zukowsky, John, and Robbe Pierce Stimson. *Hudson Valley Villas*. New York: Rizzoli, 1986.

Edith Wharton Restoration, Inc.
P.O. Box 974
Lenox, Mass. 01240
(413) 637-1899

The Edith Wharton Society
Department of English
Long Island University
Brooklyn, N.Y. 11201

The Vanderbilt Mansion
519 Albany Post Road
Hyde Park, N.Y. 12538
(914) 229-9115

The Mills Mansion
Staatsburg, N.Y.
(914) 889-8321

The Preservation Society of Newport County
P.O. Box 510
Newport, R.I. 02840
(401) 847-1000

Index

Illustration Credits

Numbers refer to page numbers.

Pavillon Colombe, St. Brice-sous-Forêt